Ghosts of Barlinnie

Ten Men
Ten Murder Trials
Ten Executions

By James Carron

Amenta Publishing
www.amentapublishing.co.uk

Ghosts of Barlinnie

Ten Men – 10 Murder Trials – 10 Executions

By James Carron

First published 2012 by Amenta Publishing

Copyright © James Carron 2012

The right of James Carron to be identified as the author of this work has been asserted by him in accordance with the Copyright, Designs and Patents Act 1988.

All rights reserved. No part of this publication may be reproduced, stored in a retrieval system, or transmitted in any form, or by any means, electronic, mechanical, photocopying, recording or otherwise, without permission in writing from the publisher.

Contents

Introduction	4
Barlinnie Prison	5
The Hanging Shed & Condemned Cell	6
1. John Lyon	16
2. Patrick Carraher	25
3. John Caldwell	36
4. Paul Christopher Harris	42
5. James Ronald Robertson	52
6. James Smith	63
7. Patrick Gallacher Deveney	72
8. George Francis Shaw	79
9. Peter Manuel	88
10. Anthony Joseph Miller	103
Postscript	115
Acknowledgements	117

Introduction

Ten men each took eight steps across the gallery of Barlinnie Prison's D-Hall, a final short walk from the grim confines of the condemned cell to the scaffold. Their time had finally come. Convicted of capital murder, each man faced the ultimate punishment – death by judicial hanging. Their crimes ranged from gangland slayings to multiple killings. The legal process exhausted and all bids for clemency rejected, the hangman's noose was primed and ready to despatch swift justice.

*****

Barlinnie Prison

Plans for a new prison at Barlinnie were drawn up in the late 19th century in a bid to ease overcrowding within Glasgow's ageing Victorian jails. Prior to 1840 there were eight prisons in the city but the number had dwindled to just two, one in Duke Street – the North Prison – and one at Glasgow Green – the South Prison.

In 1879, land on Barlinnie Farm Estate, near the town of Riddrie on the northeastern edge of the city, was bought and work began on a new four-block stronghold designed to accommodate 800 prisoners.

The first building – A-Hall – was competed in 1882 and Barlinnie received its initial batch of prisoners – three men in all – on August 15 of that year. The population grew quickly and, using prison labour to quarry and cut rock, halls B, C and D were added. A fifth block, E-Hall, was added in 1896, swelling the total capacity to 1000.

With the opening of D-Hall in 1892, Barlinnie was equipped to carry out judicial hangings. A condemned cell and execution chamber were incorporated into the design.

Barlinnie took over the role from the prison in Duke Street, where the last execution had taken place on August 3, 1928. It would be 1946 before the new gallows was christened.

*****

The Hanging Shed & Condemned Cell

Executions at Barlinnie – in common with those conducted throughout the United Kingdom – were clear cut and precise operations that followed a set pattern from beginning to end. The process began as soon as a prisoner was sentenced to death, when the judge presiding over the trial and conviction would set a date for the execution.

Commonly, prisoners were told that they would suffer death by hanging 'between the hours of eight o'clock and 10 o'clock forenoon' on the date set. In practice, all 10 Barlinnie executions were conducted at 8am sharp.

The condemned cell, located on the second floor of D-Hall, would be prepared for the prisoner's imminent arrival and the prison governor would order the execution equipment from Wandsworth Prison in London.

For each man, two execution boxes were sent north by passenger train. They were simply marked 'boxes of ropes'. One of the boxes contained the ropes, two 10 foot, six inch long lengths of three-quarter inch white Italian hemp. Generally one was brand new and the other previously used.

The second box contained leather straps, a block and tackle, a linen hood, a sandbag, a measuring rod, a piece of chalk, a length of copper wire and a pack of thread.

These were stored in the execution suite to await the arrival of the hangman and his assistant.

At this stage in the process there was no guarantee the hanging would take place on the scheduled date, or it may be cancelled altogether. Appeals generally resulted in the date being pushed back and there was always the possibility of a reprieve from the King or Queen of the day.

Once in the condemned cell, the prisoner was accompanied at all times by two prisoner officers assigned to death-watch duties.

Six officers drawn from other jails in Scotland worked a shift pattern. During the day the shifts were four hours in length while at night they were eight hours. Under Scottish Home Department rules, guards could only spend a maximum of four weeks on such duties.

One day's special leave with pay was granted to officers who were present at an execution while wardens who escorted a man to the scaffold were granted the remainder of the day off.

The prisoner spent most of his time in the cell, taking his meals there but he was allowed out for periods of exercise, an hour in the morning and an hour in the afternoon.

Prisoners dressed in prison clothing up until the day of the execution, when they wore their own civilian clothing, minus any neckwear.

The Barlinnie governor and chaplain visited the condemned man at least once a day and the medical officer visited him twice a day.

He was also allowed one visit a day by relatives or friends, which took place in the prison visiting room, plus visits from his lawyer. The prisoner was also allowed to send and receive letters.

During his time in the cell, the condemned man was kept out of sight of the rest of the prison population. Two officers accompanied him whenever he left the cell, for visits and exercise. When the prisoner required a bath, the rest of the hall had to be locked down so other inmates could not see him being moved to the washroom. He was shaved and had his hair trimmed by an officer.

At Barlinnie, condemned prisoners were allowed to sit in the vestry with the door ajar during religious services.

Prisoners were allowed 10 cigarettes, or half an ounce of tobacco a day, unless otherwise approved by the medical officer. Supplies were held by the watching officers and were released as and when required.

To help the condemned man pass the time, warders would chat with him. At Barlinnie the officers were required to 'keep the prisoner's mind occupied with talk and games when he is not reading or sleeping'. He was not allowed to go to bed during the day unless approved by the medical officer.

Cards, dominos, chess and draughts were available and the prisoner was allowed books and other reading materials although any reference to his case was removed from newspapers.

The condemned cell was twice as large as the other cells at Barlinnie to accommodate the watch officers.

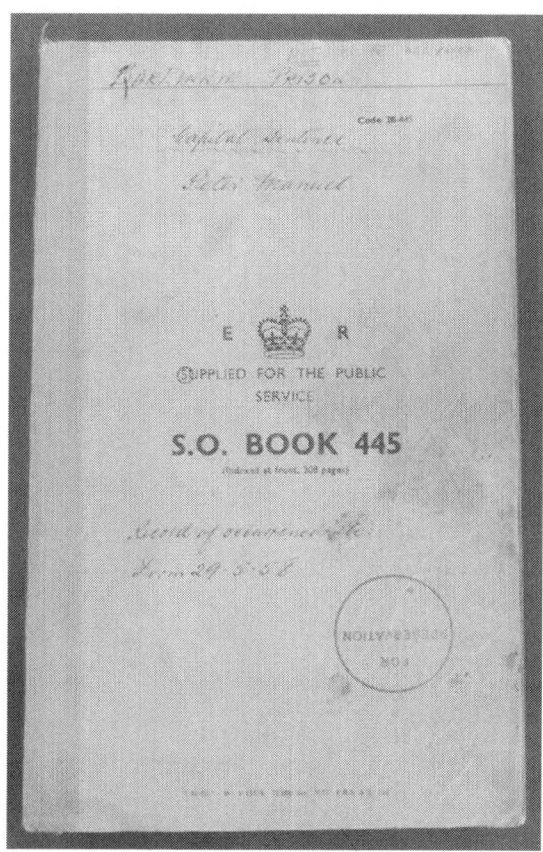

Peter Manuel's Record of Occurrence Book

A record of proceedings and conversations in the cell, along with details of letters sent and received and visits, was kept in the Condemned Cell Record of Occurrence Book, also known as the Death Watch Book.

Information logged included the times the prisoner went to bed and awoke, how he slept, how he passed his time, meals and food left, times of exercise and any other significant incidents or conversations. Everything said had to be within earshot of the wardens. The only exception to this was conversations between the prisoner and chaplain.

Warders would add their observations to this at the end of their shift and the governor would study the book's contents each morning.

Of the 10 men hanged at Barlinnie, eight appealed their original convictions and none were successful. Once a legal appeal was dismissed, a new execution date was set. In the intervening period, a plea for a reprieve could be made to the Secretary of State for Scotland.

With the new date in place, the Barlinnie governor would make arrangements to hire a hangman and an assistant executioner. The Home Office provided a list of approved candidates. He would also order a coffin and make arrangements for a local builder to come to the prison to dig a grave.

The hangman and his aide would arrive at the prison on the morning of the day prior to the execution, giving them time to inspect the equipment, which was set up by a prison engineer, and make the necessary measurements and observations.

At Barlinnie, the execution suite, colloquially known as the 'hanging shed', was a three-level chamber located just across the gallery from the condemned cell. It had double wooden doors, above which the number '29' was painted on the stone lintel. A metal ladder pinned to the wall linked the three rooms vertically.

On the top floor was the beam from which the chains, rope and noose were suspended. It was designed to do multiple executions, three at a time. The ropes were lowered through square holes in the floor.

Square holes through which the ropes were lowered

The prisoner would enter the level below where he would stand in the centre of a trapdoor and the noose would be attached. On the ground floor, below the trapdoor, there was a mortuary slab. Prior to an execution, sand was spread across the floor to catch and absorb any bodily fluids or excrement.

At Barlinnie, as with other judicial hangings in the UK at the time, the 'long drop' method was used. It was designed to break the prisoner's neck by allowing him to fall a pre-determined distance. At the end of this, he was brought up with a sharp jerk by the rope.

The noose was lined with calf leather to reduce marking to the skin and it was held in place with a rubber washer that was placed under the left side of the jaw.

At the end of the drop, the body continued to accelerate under the force of gravity but the head was constrained by the noose. With the rubber washer correctly placed, the downward momentum threw the head back, breaking the neck between the second and third vertebrae. This crushed or severed the spinal cord causing instant unconsciousness and rapid death. This is known as hyper flexion of the neck.

The phrenic nerve, which controls the diaphragm, emerges between the third and fourth vertebrae and if the fracture occurred above the fourth vertebrae the prisoner stopped breathing immediately.

It was only in the last six inches or so of the drop that the neck and vertebrae were physical damaged as the rope constricted and death occurred within a fraction of a second.

The executioners were provided with details of the height and weight of the prisoner, but they liked to see the prisoner so they could get their own idea of his dimensions. At Barlinnie this was often done when the condemned man was exercising.

The length of drop required was based upon the prisoner's weight in his clothes, combined with the hangman's experience and observations. A drop table, issued by the Home Office in 1913, was used to calculate the length required.

A chalk line was applied to the noose end of the rope marking the point where the internal circumference was 18 inches, equivalent to the circumference of the neck plus the distance from the eyelet to the top of the head after the drop. The 18-inch figure allowed for the subsequent constriction of the neck.

From the chalk line the executioner measured along the rope and tied a piece of thread at the calculated drop distance. The rope was then attached to the shackle at the end of the chain hanging down from the beam.

The chain was adjusted so that the thread mark was at the same height as the top of the prisoner's head.

The rope was then stretched prior to the hanging. A sandbag of approximately the same weight at the prisoner was attached to the end of the line, lowered through the trapdoor and left suspended over night. This removed any tendency for the rope to stretch during the actual hanging which would have reduced the force applied to the neck.

The following morning the sandbag was removed, the trap doors reset and the rope re-adjusted to get the thread mark back to the correct height.

An accurately calculated drop was said to lessen the prisoner's physical suffering and made the whole process far less traumatic for the officials called to witness the event.

On the day of the execution, the prisoner would rise at 6am and dress in his own clothing. At 6.55am he was served breakfast.

Across the landing, at 7am, the executioner took down the sandbag, adjusted the rope and placed wooden battens across the trapdoor for the attending officers to stand on.

At 7.30am, the prison chaplain visited the cell and conducted a short religious ceremony and the medical officer gave the prisoner a glass of whisky.

At 7.40am, two Baillies – civic government officers similar to magistrates – and either the town clerk or depute town – arrived at the prison. The Baillies signed a requisition for the prisoner and the governor signed a form confirming delivery. The Baillies signed a receipt for the prisoner before the governor escorted the party to the execution suite.

At 7.59am the executioner entered the condemned cell where he strapped the prisoner's arms by his side. The watch officers then led the prisoner out on to the landing where one of the Baillies would confirm the condemned man's name and ask whether he had anything to say. Any response was noted.

The prisoner was then led into the execution chamber – a distance of around eight steps from the condemned cell – and while the Baillies and the other witnesses took their positions, the executioner guided the prisoner on to the trapdoor. He stood one foot on either side of the down stroke of a letter 'T' marked in chalk on the centre of the hatch. Officers stood on the wooden battens on either side of the prisoner to steady him while the executioner placed first a hood over his head and then slipped the noose round his neck. The rope sat over the hood to prevent it blowing off in the rising draught created when the trapdoor opened. The prisoner's legs were also strapped together at the ankles.

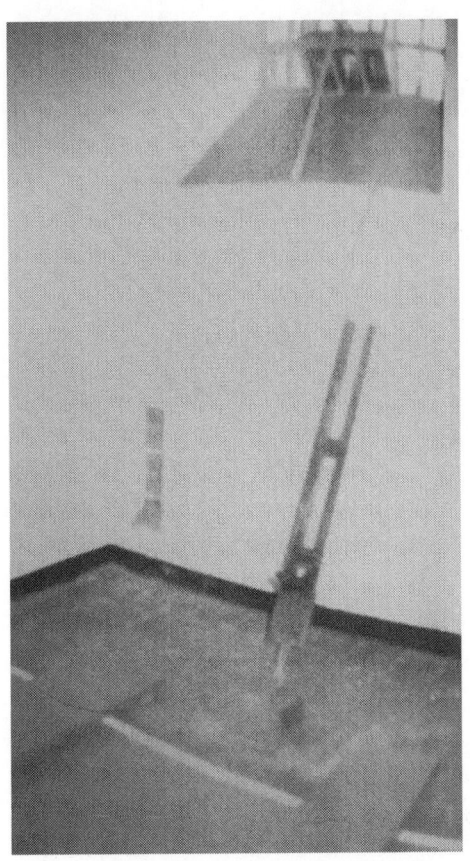

The trapdoor and lever

In addition to the prisoner, the executioner and his assistant and the two prison officers, there were six other people in attendance in the execution chamber at this point. This group of observers consisted of Barlinnie's governor, chaplain and chief medical officer, the two Baillies and either the town clerk or depute town clerk. Their role was to witness the execution, a procedure required by law.

The guards stepped back, the executioner threw a lever opening the trapdoor and the prisoner fell to his death. The whole process, from condemned cell to death, was concluded in a minute or two.

The chief medical officer would then confirm death and the body was left hanging for one hour. In the governor's office, the medical officer signed the death certificate and all of the witnesses signed in triplicate a declaration stating that sentence had been executed.

The governor then sent a short telegram to the Secretary of State for Scotland confirming the execution and between 10 and 15 minutes after the hanging a printed Notice of Execution of Sentence of Death was pinned to the front gate of the prison declaring that 'sentence of death was this day executed'. There followed the names of the six witnesses. Unlike at Duke Street Prison, a black flag was never flown above Barlinnie on execution days.

A date was set for a short judicial inquiry – heard in public – that formally concluded matters.

After the body had hung for an hour, it was re-examined by the chief medical officer and the hangman and his assistant were then responsible for taking it down and placing it on the mortuary slab. From there it was transferred fully clothed into a coffin and the casket was sealed. For a period quicklime, thought to speed the decomposition process, was poured into the coffin but this practice was discontinued in 1950.

Following a judicial hanging, the body became the property of the State. There was no question of it being returned to the deceased's family or relatives. By law it had to be interred within the grounds of the prison.

At Barlinnie, the coffin was conveyed from the execution chamber to an area of ground adjacent to the external wall of D-Hall where it was placed into the ground.

For a number of years the initials of the dead men were carved on the wall above the graves. Later these were removed, although no one knows who by or why.

At 2.30pm, the governor attended the Registrar's Office in Glasgow, delivering the death certificate and signing the official registers.

Having tidied the gallows and packed the equipment back into the execution boxes the hangman and his assistant were free to leave the prison.

The boxes were sealed – the keys were forwarded separately by post – and despatched by train to London where they were checked and prepared for their next job.

*****

1. John Lyon

A silent crowd of around 50 people gathered in the chill morning air for the first judicial hanging to be carried out at Barlinnie Prison. The solemn crowd would not see the events themselves unfold – the last public execution had taken place in Glasgow Green in 1865 – but they felt compelled to be there none-the-less. They could only imagine the grim scene being played out within the secretive execution chamber, or 'hanging shed', as it was known.

Behind the solid stone walls of the bleak Victorian institution 21-year-old Glasgow labourer John Lyon was preparing to meet his maker. Convicted of his part in the gang murder of a young seaman, he witnessed his two co-accused cheat death, last minute reprieves sparing their sorry lives. Lyon was not so lucky. He alone would go to the gallows.

At 6am he woke, dressed and was served breakfast by the prison guards assigned to watch over him. A Baillie visited him briefly to see if he had any last words to utter before the prison chaplain, the Rev John Campbell, conducted a short religious service within the confines of the cell.

At 8am, the guards led Lyon across the gallery of D-Hall and through the double doors of the execution chamber.

In a final letter to his wife Margaret, penned two days earlier, he wrote: 'Just a few lines to let you know that I have kept my chin up but it seems that my luck is out. So I am the one that has to suffer for it is so when Friday morning comes I am prepared to walk to the scaffold like a man so that you can say that your husband wasn't afraid when it came his turn.'

He kept his word. He was quiet and composed throughout.

As the doors close behind him, Lyon stepped on to the wooden trap door in the centre of the room. The guards, standing on boards either side, steadied him as executioner Thomas Pierrepoint eased a sack over his head and secured the noose firmly around his neck.

The guards stepped back and in a precise and well-rehearsed manoeuvre, Pierrepoint swung the trap door level, sending Lyon to his death at two minutes past eight o'clock on the morning of February 8, 1946.

Less than a quarter of an hour later, a warder pinned a printed notice to the front gates of the prison.

It read: 'We, the undersigned, hereby declare that sentence of death was this day executed on John Lyon, in the prison of Barlinnie, Glasgow, in our presence.'

Below, the note bore the signatures of six witnesses, Baillies James R. Duff and Hugh Fraser; Depute Town Clerk Robert Richmond; Prison Governor Joseph P. Mayo; Medical Officer George M. Scott; and John M.C. Campbell, Prison Chaplain.

Moments earlier a telegram was sent to the Scottish Office in Edinburgh. It read simply: 'Lyon executed – Governor, Barlinnie Prison'.

The waiting crowd queue to read the Notice of Execution of Sentence of Death

In an orderly line, the waiting crowd queued up to read the notice before dispersing in an equally poised fashion from the prison grounds.

Barlinnie's first judicial hanging came 17 years after the last execution to be held in Glasgow's Duke Street Prison, when George Reynolds was sentenced to death for the murder of a workmate in a city bakery.

Lyon's death was intended to send a stern message to the gangs of Glasgow, whatever their religious or political affiliations, that such aggressive and unruly behaviour would not be tolerated. As a deterrent, however, it failed and the city continued to be plagued by a culture of mob violence for decades to come.

Lyon was a member of the Crosbie Clan, small time crooks who were well known in the Govanhill district of the city where they made a good living terrorising and extorting money from shopkeepers.

Lyon was married to Margaret Crosbie and the couple shared a house in Jamieson Street with her brothers, Hugh, Robert and Alexander Crosbie. The brothers were career criminals. Despite a troubled school life, Lyon was a grafter and, for a time at least, he had worked for a living. He was no angel, though. He had seven previous convictions for theft, breach of the peach, assault and assaulting a police officer.

Born in Alloa in 1924, he attended a local school. At the age of 10, he was sent to Dale Approved School in Arbroath. Described as 'backward' by his teachers, he spent six years at the special school before leaving to work in the coalmines. After a year down the pits, he moved on to travelling shows before being called up to the Army at the age of 20. He was discharged from military service after only 10 weeks.

Three weeks later he embarked upon a journey that would end on the Barlinnie scaffold.

On the night of October 20, 1945, Alexander and Hugh Crosbie and Lyon were out on the town. Armed with knives, bayonets and other weapons, they were spoiling for a fight and it wasn't long before they found their first potential target.

At around 10.30pm, 19-year-old Joseph Smith, a member of a gang called the Dougie Boys, was standing chatting to two girls and another youth at Douglas Corner, the meeting point of Douglas Street – from which the gang took its name – and Argyle Street.

Govan Cross

They were approached by a group of eight young men – including Lyon and the two Crosbie boys. Spotting weapons and knowing that only trouble lay ahead, Smith bolted.

The baying mob gave chase, pursuing Smith through the streets. He jumped on to a stationary tramcar but immediately leapt back off, running round the front of the vehicle in an attempt to evade the gang. He raced down Brown Street and made it safely home.

Two witnesses, a couple living in Brown Street, later told police that everyone in the pursuing gang was brandishing a weapon. One youth held aloft a small revolver, they said.

They were shouting: 'If anyone wants it, they can get it'.

With Smith lost, the gang regrouped at a coffee stall in Jamaica Street where one of them, Alexander Lennie, showed off a bayonet. With equal bravado, Alexander Crosbie held a bayonet to the throat of another man.

Eager to continue their rampage, the group boarded a passing tram, heading west to Washington Street where they all got off. Troubled flared up again as the group pelted the vehicle with bottles.

In full cry, they tore down Washington Street, chasing 19-year-old demobilised sailor John Brady, who was out looking for his younger brother Joe at the time. It is thought the gang mistook Brady for Joseph Smith, the lad they had earlier terrorised at Douglas Corner.

Alone, Brady stood little chance. The mob was soon upon him, dragging him to the ground in a feverish flurry of blows and stabs. They battered and cut him so badly he died instantly.

Leaving Brady lying on his back, his blood-spattered head rolling in the gutter, the gang fled down Washington Street. However, they were forced to double back to avoid police officers at the bottom of the street.

A post mortem conducted the following morning revealed that Brady suffered bruising and lesions to his face and head but the fatal blow, dealt early in the attack, was a knife wound to his back. The blade passed through the back wall of the chest, cut into his heart and punctured his lung. In all, there were 16 knife wounds on his body most inflicted by what the pathologist later described in court as a 'long knife'. The attack was classic Glasgow gang violence.

Later that day, police officers raided the Crosbie home in Jamieson Street and arrested Alexander, Hugh and Robert Crosbie and Lyon. Elsewhere in Govanhill, they picked up a man named Patrick Houston (27), suspecting he was also part of the gang.

All five men were charged with the murder of Brady and remanded to Barlinnie Prison to await trial. Before the case came to court, Robert Crosbie and Patrick Houston were released after their alibis checked out.

However, another man, Alexander Lennie (25), from Paisley, was arrested in connection with the incident

Eight weeks later, Lyon, Lennie and Alexander and Hugh Crosbie stood side by side in the dock at the High Court in Glasgow, facing Lord MacKay and a jury of nine men and six women.

The first charge against the four men alleged that on October 20, 1945, in Argyle Street, Brown Street, Crimea Street, Carrick Street and Washington Street, they conducted themselves in a disorderly manner, used threatening and abusive language, brandished bayonets and other weapons, challenged others to fight and threatened to assault them with bayonets and other weapons.

The second charge alleged that in Argyle Street, Crimea Street and Carrick Street, they assaulted a man, chased him through the streets and attempted to punch him and strike him with bayonets and other weapons.

The third and final charge alleged that in Washington Street, they assaulted Thomas Brady, cut him and stabbed him repeatedly on the body, head and face with bayonets and other weapons and did murder him.

All four men denied being members of any gang and lodged special defences of alibi. The Crosbie brothers and Lyon claimed they were in and out of each other's company during the course of the night but never left Govanhill. All were home eating fish and chips shortly after 11pm.

Lennie admitted that he was on the tramcar with a large group of disorderly men but said he did not get off at Washington Street, travelling on to Finnieston Street, some distance away.

On December 15, after a trial lasting five days, the jury took just one hour to reach a conclusion. They found Lyon, Lennie and Alexander Crosbie guilty of the murder of Thomas Brady. They returned a not proven verdict on Hugh Crosbie on the charge of murder. All four men were convicted on the other two charges.

Hugh Crosbie was sentenced to three years in prison. Lyon, Lennie and Alexander Crosbie braced themselves for a much graver fate. Lord MacKay sentenced all three to death.

The *Glasgow Citizen* reported that none of the accused appeared to show any emotion as they were sentenced. As the men left the dock there was a round of applause from the gallery to which one of them turned and replied: 'Happy New Year'.

They were despatched to the condemned cell at Barlinnie to await execution, which was scheduled for January 5, 1946. However, appeals were promptly lodged, forcing a postponement.

On January 21, 1946, the appeals of all three men were dismissed. In their summing up, the appeal court judges noted: 'In the three cases now under review it is necessary to keep in mind that at the present time there is considerable lawlessness in certain parts of Glasgow, that assaults, whether in concert or singly, are not uncommon and that the police are perturbed about the position.

'If these three men are reprieved the police may well feel discouraged in their concerted attack on this crime situation in parts of Glasgow at the present time.

'The crime was a cowardly assault by a number of men on one defenceless youth who never had a chance. There is no question of provocation.'

The Lord Justice General remarked: 'When people brandish lethal weapons, and a man is done to death with many blows and many injuries, then those people who have been brandishing the weapons are guilty of the crime of killing. There may be other questions, but so far as I see no evidence of other than murder. There is considerable evidence of the greatest intimidation and brutality.'

At the time, appeals were rarely successful and it marked the end of the road for the trio as far as the Scottish legal system was concerned. Their only hope of escaping the noose was a reprieve and pleas were duly made to the Secretary of State for Scotland who had the power to intervene and recommend to the King that he might consider leniency.

On this front, there was good news for Lennie and Crosbie. On February 5, the Secretary of State advised the King to 'remit the sentences of death passed upon Crosbie and Lennie on condition of their serving sentences of life imprisonment'.

Lennie's reprieve was partly due to new information that had come to light after the trial while Crosbie was spared on the grounds of youth. He 'celebrated' his 18th birthday on the day he was convicted.

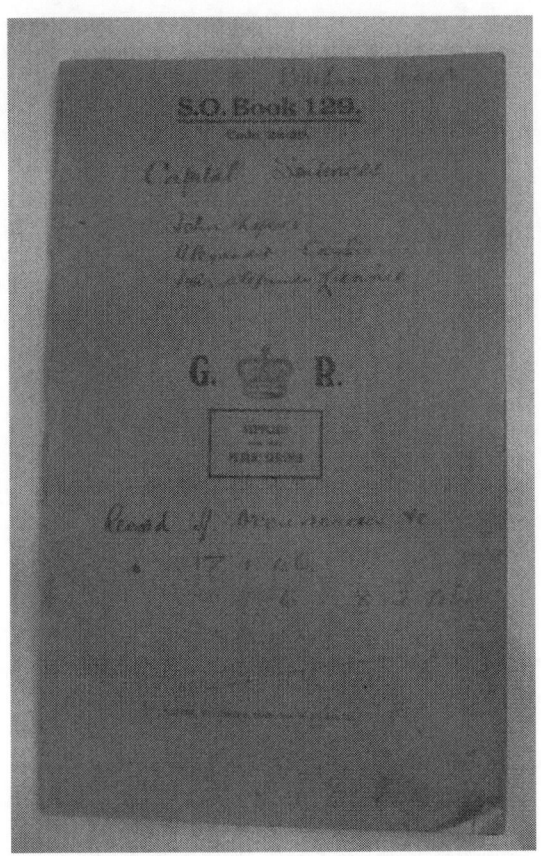

John Lyon's Condemned Cell Record of Occurrence Book

Lyon, however, was not so fortunate and he returned to the condemned cell alone to see out the remainder of his days. In a letter to his father, he wrote on February 6: 'We had a raw deal right from the start but that's the law.'

Arrangements for death watching duties were drawn up by the prison governor and approved. Two prison officers would be in attendance in the cell day and night while an additional officer was added to the night patrol. The governor also rubber stamped the issue of up to 20 cigarettes a day for Lyon.

Boxes containing the execution equipment were already at the prison. They had been ordered following the passing of the death sentence on the three men and sent up by train from Wandsworth Prison in London. There were six boxes in all, two for each hanging.

Government documents reveal that expenses associated with the execution included the cost of transporting the boxes (£4, 4s) plus outlays for a soda siphon (2s 10d) and 'beer for the executioner' (2s 8d).

Ahead of his death, Lyon wrote to the prison governor thanking officers for their 'kind attention' during his stay at Barlinnie.

He added: 'I feel in my heart that I have not had a fair deal in not getting a reprieve along with the other two men who were sentenced with me.'

He did, however, remain optimistic and on the eve of his execution he was still hopeful of a reprieve. He joked with his guards that he wanted to postpone the time of the hanging so he could have 'another two hours in bed'.

Even on the morning of his walk to the scaffold he said there was still time for 'the messages to come'.

Unfortunately for Lyon no messages came and on February 8, 1946, the *Edinburgh Evening Dispatch* reported: 'A small crowd of people began to gather on the driveway leading to Barlinnie Prison as soon as it turned light.

'By eight o'clock, the hour of the execution, the crowd had increased to 50. From the outside there was no sign of the drama that was taking place inside the prison walls.

'At exactly 8.05am on the prison clock, which could be seen from the driveway, two officers emerged through a small doorway in the main gate and proceeded to fasten the official intimation of execution on the door.'

Onlookers were not permitted to read the notice until 8.30am, by which time the Baillies and depute town clerk had left the prison by a private road.

In the condemned cell, Lyon left behind a tie, handkerchief, two rings, a fountain pen, army pay book, comb, toothbrush, toothpaste, two photographs and four letters. Not much to show for a young life.

*****

2. Patrick Carraher

In a city accustomed to decades of gang fighting, Patrick Carraher was a lone warrior, a loose cannon with no religious or political affiliations. Dubbed the Fiend of the Gorbals, he was branded a persistent and dangerous criminal by police with no allegiance to anyone other than himself.

While the gangs of Glasgow, the likes of the Protestant Billy Boys and the Catholic Norman Conks, adhered to a code – they targeted their sworn enemies and left the ordinary man in the street alone – Carraher was less discerning. Anyone was fair game for this psychopathic hard man who loved violence and inflicting pain on others. He was a career criminal who stabbed and slashed his way through life.

Carraher was born into a decent working class family in 1906. He attended St Luke's School until he was 14 and was described by his teachers as an average scholar.

After leaving school he worked briefly as a message boy for a butcher but soon became mixed up with a gang known as the Southside Stickers. Despite his tender years, he was indoctrinated into the tribe and it was not long before he came to the attention of the city police.

In January 1923 – aged just 17 – Carraher was arrested on a charge of theft and assault. He was sent to prison for 14 days but a month later he was back in court where he was found guilty of theft.

In March of the same year, following a spate of thefts from shops, he was sentenced to two years' detention in a borstal. Soon after he was released he was returned for another year after failing to change his ways.

But again, he was back out on the streets and up to his old tricks. Seven prison sentences ranging in length from four month to two years followed for a plethora of offences including theft, housebreaking and possession of explosives. It was all in the line of duty for a man who made his living from crime.

Patrick Carraher

With his list of previous convictions growing, Carraher had no qualms about being sent down. The brutal regime of prison life excited him and he revelled in the violence that frequently erupted behind bars. He enjoyed a fight and there was plenty of that in the jail.

There were clearly times, however, where he was not so content with his lot. In 1934, following a prison disturbance in which he was involved he slashed his own throat. He recovered from the self-inflicted injury but it left him with a large scar across his neck.

As he grew older and more hardened to the ways of the world, Carraher began to drink heavily and soon became an alcoholic. This, coupled with his quick temper and callous disregard for society, made for a lethal cocktail. And it was a young soldier on leave who would bear the brunt.

On the night of August 13, 1938, Carraher was reeling after a girl he dated, Kate Morgan, ended the relationship abruptly. Very drunk, he spotted one of her friends, Margaret Nicol, out walking in the street with her boyfriend, James Durie.

Carraher confronted the couple at Gorbals Cross and began swearing at Nicol, demanding she tell Morgan he wanted to see her. Threats followed and Durie stepped in to defend his girl. Carraher grabbed the young man's jacket and pushed him back against a wall. He whipped out a knife and challenged Durie to a fight.

Seeing the knife, Durie declined the invitation and after throwing Carraher off he and his girlfriend ran away from the lumbering drunk.

Durie's older brother John soon got wind of the altercation and, accompanied by a friend, Peter Howard, the two siblings decided to confront Carraher face to face.

Gorbals Cross

When they caught up with him, he was too drunk to fight. His state of inebriation, however, did not stop him from shouting and swearing after the Duries as they walked away.

A passing serviceman, 23-year-old James Shaw intervened and told Carraher to 'shut up'. Matters should have ended at that point when a policeman appeared and ordered those present to disperse.

Carraher, Shaw and Howard, who had remained to keep the peace, did move on, but not very far. In Ballater Street, Carraher and Shaw squared up to each other once more. Howard, unable to separate the pair, decided to leave them to it but he had only walked a few yards when he turned to see Shaw staggering across the street. His hand was clutching his throat, blood spurting from between his fingers. Carraher had vanished.

Howard ran back to help the soldier. An ambulance was called but Shaw died within an hour of arriving at Glasgow Royal Infirmary.

After taking witness statements, police had enough evidence to arrest Carraher and, charged with the murder of James Shaw during the early hours of August 14, his trial got underway at the High Court in Glasgow on September 12, 1938.

Medical evidence confirmed that Shaw had been stabbed in the neck with a knife. The blade severed his jugular vein and he bled to death.

The Durie brothers and Howard all gave evidence for the prosecution, as did others who had later heard Carraher boasting about the killing.

Unfortunately for the Crown, no one had actually seen Carraher stab Shaw and no murder weapon was produced in court – Carraher had thrown the knife into the River Clyde shortly after the attack.

Defence witnesses testified that the accused had been drinking for most of the day prior to the incident and was so drunk he could hardly stand up.

After more than two hours of deliberation, the jury cleared him of murder but found him guilty of the lesser charge of culpable homicide.

Sentencing Carraher, Lord Pitman said: 'The jury has taken a lenient view of the case. I think their verdict means that they were satisfied you were under the influence of drink and had not the deliberate intent required in murder.'

Had a murder conviction been secured, Carraher would have been sentenced to death. Instead, he got three years in prison.

After serving his time, Carraher returned to Glasgow in 1941 and, with the Second World War raging, he was called up to serve King and country. The army, however, rejected the hard man, deeming him unfit for duty due to persistent stomach complaints and a bad chest. Carraher was free to roam the mean streets. He met a woman, Sarah Bonnar, and the pair set up home in Tarbet Street in the Townhead district of the city. Together they had a child.

Fatherhood did not mellow Carraher and with police numbers seriously depleted due to the war effort and a new accomplice in the form of Sarah Bonnar's brother Daniel, his violent behaviour continued virtually unhindered.

In 1943 he was arrested again and stood trial at the High Court in Glasgow on a charge of assault. Carraher was found guilty of attempting to slash a man with an open razor and he was sentenced to another three years behind bars.

Carraher was released from Peterhead Prison on May 5, 1945 and was out on licence when he committed what was to be his final and most damning criminal offence.

On the night of November 23, 1945, John Gordon, a soldier, and his two brothers Joseph and Edward and their brother-in-law Duncan Revie were out on the town. John Gordon had served 20 years with the Seaforth Highlanders and spent time incarcerated in a German prisoner of war camp. He had just returned to Scotland and he and his brother were celebrating his freedom and homecoming with more than a few drinks.

They had five or six half glasses of whisky and some beer in the Coronation Bar on the corner of Taylor Street and McAslin Street before moving on to Cameron's Bar in Rottenrow. There they drank wine and more beer and were joined by John Keatings, a deserter from the Royal Navy.

With his brothers so drunk they had passed out, John Gordon, Keatings and Revie left the bar at closing time - 9.30pm - and stood for a time on the pavement outside where they were joined by another man, John Fullerton.

Soon after Fullerton's arrival, Carraher's partner in crime, Daniel Bonnar appeared on the scene. He had a score to settle with one of John Gordon's brothers and approached the men as they stood chatting.

As John was the only member of the family to hand, Bonnar decided to have a pop at him. Fullarton advised Gordon not to get involved but Keatings and Revie promptly took up Bonnar's invitation to fight.

Bonnar had no interest in the pair and aimed his first blow at Gordon. Revie stepped in and both he and Keatings chased Bonnar down the street and cornered him. They set about Bonnar but he managed to wriggle free from their clasp and fled to his sister Sarah's house.

There he discarded his own jacket and put another on before heading out once again, this time with Carraher by his side. Carraher was armed with a razor sharp chisel, which he described as 'the very tool for them'.

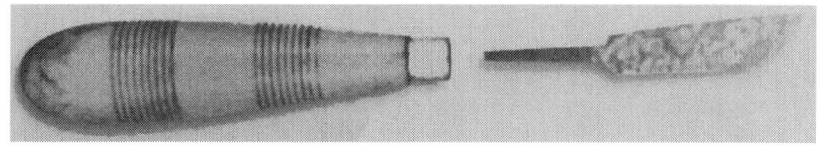

Carraher's razor sharp chisel

The pair made their way to McAslin Street where they hid in a tenement close and waited for Revie, Keatings and Gordon to come by.

Keatings had left the group and gone elsewhere. Revie and Gordon, however, were walking along Taylor Street. They were heading straight into Carraher's trap.

As the two men rounded the corner of Taylor Street and walked into McAslin Street, Carraher and Bonnar ambushed them. Carraher rushed at Gordon while Bonnar targeted Revie.

Once again, Revie got the better of Bonnar who, for a third time that night ran off. Gordon, however, was less fortunate. Carraher grabbed hold of him and Revie turned to see the man's hand rise towards the neck of his friend. Clenched in his fist, was a weapon.

Before Revie could do anything, Carraher fled, but not before he had inflicted a fatal wound. Gordon staggered and fell to the ground, blood spurting from his neck.

Revie picked the injured man up and carried him up two flights of stairs to his home in McAslin Street before running off to seek help from the Gordon brothers.

Gordon had a small wound below his left ear. Although almost insignificant on the surface, the cut was four inches deep. He was taken in a taxi to Glasgow Royal Infirmary but died within a minute of arriving.

Carraher for his part was soon boasting to anyone who would listen that he had given John Gordon 'a wee jag'.

Patrick Carraher

On February 28, Carraher once again found himself in the dock at Glasgow's High Court. He was facing his second murder charge but on this occasion the evidence was conclusive. Witnesses, including Revie, testified that they had seen him stab Gordon in the neck and Carraher's so-called friend Daniel Bonnar gave evidence against him.

The defence attempted to argue that Carraher was a person of psychopathic personality and, as a result, diminished responsibility. Doctors agreed, however, that Carraher was neither insane nor mentally deficient nor feeble minded.

He was described by psychological experts as 'callous in his outlook upon society' and someone with a very poor capacity to exercise self-control.

In his summing up, Lord Russell was of the opinion that diminished responsibility was not established in this case and the jury of nine men and six women took just 20 minutes to unanimously convict Carraher of murder. They made no recommendation for mercy and the judge sentenced him to death.

After the trial, the City of Glasgow Police described Carraher as a 'persistent and dangerous criminal'.

He appealed against his conviction but this was dismissed on March 20, 1946.

Despite his character and convictions, a petition of 4500 signatures supported Carraher's plea to the Secretary of State for Scotland for a reprieve. It is more than likely, however, that the majority who signed the document were expressing their opposition to the continued presence of the death penalty, rather than any desire to save a man who had wreaked havoc and terror on the streets of Glasgow for over two decades.

Carraher may well have expected his punishment to be reduced to a life sentence. During the war, Glasgow, like many British cities, had not executed any civilians for fear it might damage public morale. Although the war was still fresh in people's minds, judicial hanging remained an integral part of the fight against crime, which had flourished at home during the conflict.

John Lyon was the first to face the hangman's noose in the post-war years and 40-year-old Carraher duly followed. Reprieve rejected, execution was set for April 6.

During his stay in the condemned cell, his partner and his sister – who pressed him to consider marrying Sarah Bonnar for the sake of the couple's child – visited Carraher. She also wanted to send him a dozen eggs. The prison governor, who said it was 'undesirable' for a prisoner to be eating food sent from the outside, rejected this. Bonnar was, however, allowed to send her lover Capstan Full Strength cigarettes.

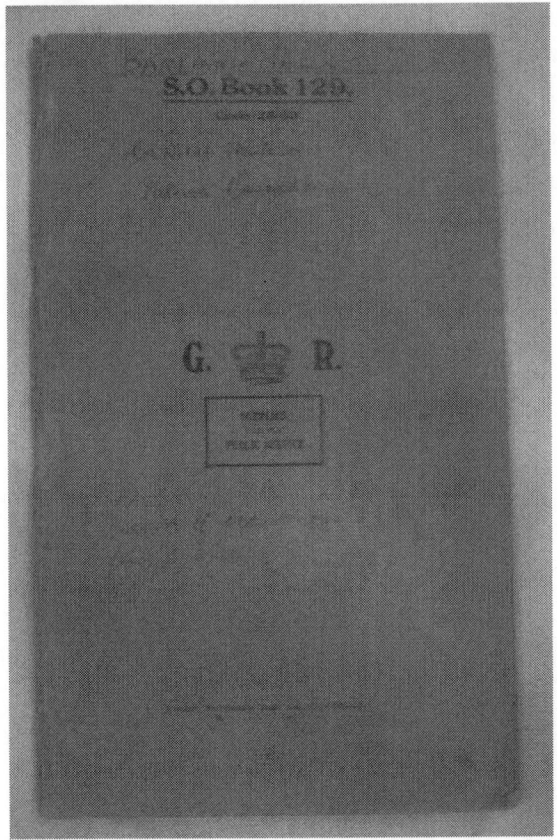

Carraher's Condemned Cell Record of Occurrence Book

Carraher kept his mind occupied played cards and dominoes. Frequently described as 'cheerful', some days he was more inclined to chat than others. When he was in the mood to converse, he talked about his past life, crimes, football and his time in Peterhead.

He knew that his appeal would be a 'washout' and said that if his reprieve failed they would 'have to drag him over the landing'.

On the day of his execution, Carraher woke at 6am, dressed in own clothing and said that he had not had too bad a night's sleep. He lay back down on his bed for a time before washing at 6.43am. He was served breakfast and although he drank tea he did not eat anything. He did, however, smoke continually.

He was described as 'cheerful and calm' as he walked to the scaffold where hangman Thomas Pierrepoint waited and, referring to the execution, was heard to remark: 'Nothing in it'.

After sending the Secretary of State for Scotland a telegram simply stating 'execution effected', prison governor Joseph Mayo had the job of returning Carraher's personal belongings to his family. These included a cap, overcoat, pullover, braces, collars, ties, handkerchiefs, shaving kit and toothbrush.

Carraher's father, also Patrick, suggested passing them on to his fiancé.

'I don't want to see them never mind claim them, so if nobody has called by the time you get this note would you kindly have them destroyed,' he wrote.

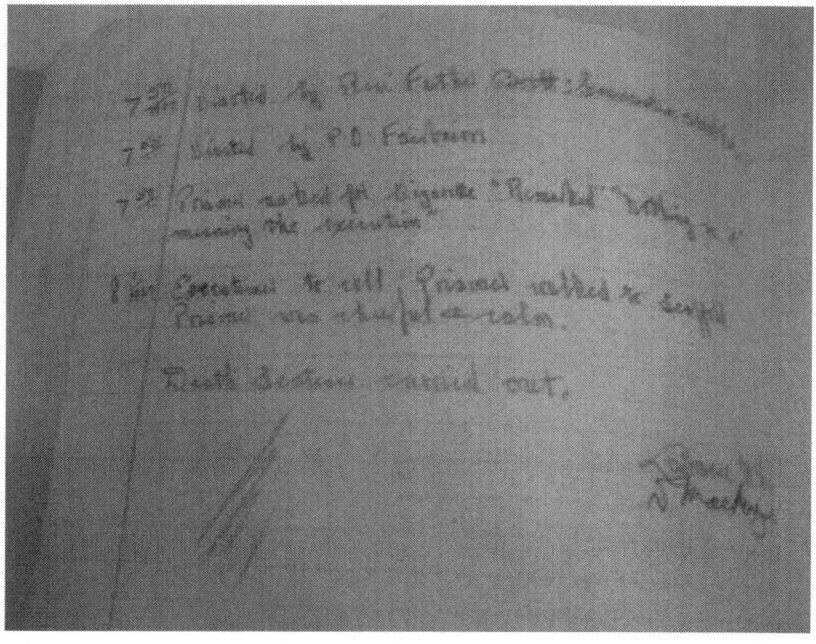

Final page in the Condemned Cell Record of Occurrence Book for Carraher

Clearly, like most of the population of Glasgow, he was glad to see the demise of the Fiend of the Gorbals. He did not want to be reminded of his son's lawless life and callous crimes.

*****

3. John Caldwell

Returning home from an evening at the cinema, James Deekan and his wife Annie were surprised to see a light on in their house. Surprise quickly turned to alarm. The property in the Carntyne district of Glasgow was empty and all the lights were off when they left.

Expecting trouble, Deekan sent his wife to fetch their neighbour James Straiton, a retired policeman.

'Tell him to bring his truncheon,' he added before cautiously creeping up the driveway towards the front door. He slipped his key into the Yale lock but it wouldn't open. The catch had clearly been put down to prevent anyone entering and disturbing those within.

Heading round to the back of the house, he found the kitchen window open. Deekan climbed in and moved stealthily through to open the front door for Straiton, pausing briefly to survey the lounge.

'The living room is in a terrible mess,' he told his neighbour in a whisper. 'Things strewn all over the floor.'

Suddenly the pair heard a noise. Deekan looked up the stairs and saw two young men bounding down towards him. He stepped back and spotted that one of the men, who wore a white scarf, was carrying a pair of pistols, one in each hand.

'Put down the guns,' Deekan shouted.

'You'd better let us through, or you'll get it,' the youth replied, pointing the guns straight at Deekan.

The two older men stood their ground and as they closed in on the intruder the youth pulled the trigger and a bullet whistled past Deekan.

Straiton raised his truncheon and hurled himself at the gunman, battering him on the head and arm. The teenager stumbled but he did not go down. He trained his gun on the former policeman and discharged two shots.

Firing at a range of between three and eight inches, the second, fatal bullet tore through Straiton's jacket and ripped into his stomach. He staggered from the front door and collapsed on to the ground. The intruder and his accomplice fled, firing shots at Deekan, who had gone to the aid of his neighbour, and his wife as they ran down the driveway and out on to Edinburgh Road.

An ambulance was called but Straiton, a former Detective Sergeant, died shortly after the shooting.

James Straiton

Straiton, who was 61 when he died, joined the Lanarkshire Police in 1903 and served with them until 1912 when he was transferred to Glasgow. He retired from the police force in 1933 after 30 years' service. Commended on 10 different occasions for devotion to duty, Glasgow's Chief Constable Malcolm McCulloch described him as a most conscientious and courageous police officer. His action on the night of his death was prompted by a high sense of citizenship, he added.

Detectives found that on the evening of March 16, 1946, the house had been entered by one of the youths who had scaled a drainpipe, breaking an upstairs window. He then let his companion in through the kitchen window.

Examining clues found at previous similar burglaries, the investigators singled out a fragment of a thumbprint and found it matched that of 19-year-old John Caldwell, a former soldier recently released from borstal.

After making good their escape, Caldwell and his 15-year-old accomplice, John Mushet, headed for the home of Caldwell's father, 57-year-old James Caldwell. They arrived there shortly after 9pm and Caldwell senior was surprised to see his son in stocking feet. The teenager admitted he lost his shoes at a house in Carntyne.

The following day, Caldwell went to see his son, taking with him a newspaper in which there was an account of the murder.

'I asked him if he had a gun,' Caldwell senior said. 'And he replied: "Aye, it's in my pocket."'

Caldwell senior took the gun from his son's coat pocket, along with rounds of ammunition, and threw them in the River Clyde.

His son told him his wrist was sore and that he had been struck on the head by a baton as he tried to get away. He added that the gun had been fired three times, once when he was hit on the head, once when he was hit on the wrist and again as he fled.

It was six days before police located and arrested Caldwell. By that time they had enough evidence to charge him with both the murder of James Straiton and a string of burglaries.

The man leading the investigation, Detective Lieutenant Robert Colquhoun, said that when cautioned and charged, Caldwell admitted: 'It was me who shot the man.'

On June 25, 1946, Caldwell's trial opened before Lord Stevenson and a jury at the High Court in Glasgow.

He was charged with breaking into a house in Elcho Street, Glasgow on February 28 and stealing clothing; breaking into a house in Whitehill Street on March 10, and stealing jewellery and £123 cash; breaking into the same house a week later and stealing a watch and £8 and also discharging a loaded firearm into the lock of a room door; breaking into a house in Golfhill Drive on March 25 and stealing jewellery and at the same place threatening to shoot a woman.

He was also charged, while acting with Mushet, with breaking into the house at 524 Edinburgh Road, Glasgow, occupied by James Deekan, and stealing a revolver and other items.

The charge further alleged that in the garden of the house he discharged a loaded firearm at Deekan and attempted to murder him and that he discharged a loaded firearm at Straiton, who lived at 528 Edinburgh Road, and shot him in the body whereby he was so severely injured that he died shortly afterwards, and did murder him.

Defence lawyer J.F. Gordon Thomson said medical evidence indicated that while Caldwell was sane he was 'not quite normal' and this had a bearing on his actions that fateful night.

After an absence of 50 minutes, the jury found Caldwell guilty of murder and the reckless discharge of firearms. They recommended mercy be shown because of his age.

Lord Stevenson, however, was less inclined to display compassion and sentenced the teenager to death. Lord Normand dismissed a subsequent appeal.

The case against John Mushet was dismissed on the grounds he was 'mentally retarded'.

Caldwell, who had previous convictions for theft and housebreaking, ran away from home at the age of 14 and spent time in borstal. He joined the army, serving with the Seaforth Highlanders, and was based for a time at Fort George barracks near Inverness.

After shooting Straiton, he attempted suicide. He said that he went home, 'hung a blanket over the scullery door, put 3d in the meter and turned on the gas.'

Finding this had no effect he drank a bottle of iodine.

It was one of a number of claims he made to guards assigned to watch over him in the condemned cell at Barlinnie.

While his father had disposed of one of the guns in the Clyde, Caldwell stated that he had hidden the other one – which he bought for £4 – and would retrieve it when he was released from prison.

He showed no remorse for his victim, saying he was 'not at all sorry for Straiton or his family' and he added that he wished he had 'fixed up' Deekan.

He also said that if he had known Straiton was dead he would have shot his co-accused as well so nobody would be able to identify him. Caldwell harboured the belief that it was Mushet who was responsible for the police finding and arresting him.

He passed his time in Barlinnie reading library books, including the bible, and playing cards.

Caldwell also displayed a keen interest in his fate. On one occasion during exercise he asked the officers accompanying him what kind of headdress he would have to wear for the execution. He asked whether or not he would see his executioner. On another occasion he asked where the gallows were and later pointed out where his grave would be.

The Condemned Cell Occurrence Book reveals that Caldwell was usually cheerful, even after being informed that his appeal had been dismissed. He was hopeful of success, saying it was 'better doing 15 years in prison than swinging'.

It was a different matter when his plea for a reprieve was rejected. The book reveals that he took it 'very bad'. His face was very white and he was very unsteady on his legs, one watch officer wrote. Later he said he would try and 'take it like a man and be brave.'

Caldwell had earlier dreamed that he got a reprieve and said if his reprieve wasn't granted 'his ghost would wander round Barlinnie Prison'.

On the eve of execution, he was served fish and chips for supper. He wrote three letters and spent some of the evening doing card tricks with the prison chaplain. At 7.30pm he was given a glass of whisky and he later retired to bed for the final time.

The following morning, he rose at 6am and, after a short service conducted by the chaplain, he was served a breakfast of porridge and milk, bread and bacon, egg and fish.

At 7.14am, he was given a whisky and he then showed one of the watch officers a card trick that the chaplain demonstrated the previous evening.

The Condemned Cell Occurrence Book described Caldwell as cheerful and composed, stating that he chatted with prison officers in the time leading up to his death sentence.

At 8am, after asking so many questions about his execution, he finally met Albert Pierrepoint. It was but a brief acquaintance; two minutes later he was dead, his lifeless corpse swinging from the end of a rope.

Among his personal possessions, his army uniform of battle dress blouse, trousers and coat, were returned to the Seaforth Highlanders at Maryhill Barracks, Glasgow.

While Caldwell was 'not at all sorry for Straiton or his family', the people of Glasgow – in particular his fellow officers – were and they rallied round, raising what *The Glasgow Herald* reported as a 'considerable sum' of money for his widow.

On November 12, 1946, the Chief Constable presented three cheques to her. The first represented the proceeds of a football match and a variety and cinema show organised by Glasgow police. The second was the result of donations made by police officers from all over Scotland, and the third was from cops in Glasgow.

*****

4. Paul Christopher Harris

There can be no more noble a sacrifice than laying down one's life for a friend or loved one. In the case of brothers Paul and Claude Harris, there was nothing noble about the circumstances that led to them facing such a tough life or death decision. But, in a thoroughly dignified manner, the younger of the two men gave up his life to let his brother live.

Twenty eight-year-old Paul and 30-year-old Claude Harris – known throughout Govan as the 'inseparable Harrises' – ended up sharing the condemned cell at Barlinnie following a brawl in which another man perished. It was the culmination of a night of alcohol-fuelled violence.

From the outset, it looked as if the pair would remain joined at the hip to the end, taking their final walk to the scaffold together. But at the last minute, Paul confessed that he alone struck the fatal blow. Whether or not this was the case, it had the desired effect and the elder sibling was spared the gallows.

'A life has been taken and I'm giving mine in return,' Paul said. 'That should satisfy the world and let Claude go on living.'

Their path to prison started in a public house in Glasgow's Orkney Street on the evening of July 7, 1950. The two were drinking heavily with a pair of friends, one of them Walter Drennan, when a fight broke out over a woman.

One of the four picked up a glass and smashed it into the face of another drinker, Patrick Clark, severely injuring him. With Clark bleeding heavily, the men quickly left the pub and headed for the Harris home at 155 Neptune Street. However, on their way there they stopped off at a tenement a few blocks away and there the fighting continued. The incident may have stemmed from the clash in the pub but was more likely gang related. Neptune Street was one of the roughest and most rundown neighbourhoods in Govan and clashes between rival mobs – usually sectarian fights between

Protestant and Catholic groups – were common. Poverty was rife and with unemployment high many young men spent their time hanging around on street corners or drinking in the district's many pubs.

Neptune Street

A resident of 151 Neptune Street, Francis Murray, was attacked. He was punched on the face and body, knocked to the ground and repeatedly kicked. Another man, Richard Boyle, was hit in the face with a bottle.

With two men already down, the orgy of violence continued unabated and was soon to take a fatal twist. The brothers and their accomplices turned their attentions to Martin Dunleavy, who also lived in Neptune Street. One of the men smashed another bottle against the wall and thrust the remaining shards of glass deep into Dunleavy's chest and face. They knocked him to the ground and delivered a severe kicking.

With blood gushing from a zigzag wound that stretched from his cheek to his chin and was so deep that his tonsils were visible through the gash, an ambulance was called and the bruised and battered Dunleavy was conveyed to Glasgow's Southern General Hospital.

Once doctors patched him up, Police Constable James Ross interviewed Dunleavy in his hospital bed but he refused to divulge the names of his attackers.

He reportedly told the officer: 'I know the bastards but I'm not telling you. I'll get them myself.'

The 38-year-old did not live to extract his revenge. He died a few hours later following a massive haemorrhage.

However, the police had other witnesses, including Dunleavy's two pals who were injured in the Neptune Street attacks, and there was sufficient evidence to arrest the Harris brothers and Walter Drennan.

Paul Harris

Towards the end of September the trio appeared before Lord Thomson at the High Court in Glasgow. All three men faced three charges of assault and one of assault and murder. They all pled not guilty and claimed that they had acted in self-defence.

At the end of the four-day trial the jury returned after deliberating for an hour and 40 minutes. They found Paul and Claude Harris guilty of murder but made a strong recommendation for mercy. Ironically, Drennan, who Lord Thomson described as the 'ringleader' in the assault on Dunleavy, was found not guilty of his murder. He was sentenced to a year in jail after being convicted of assaulting Francis Murray.

Paul Harris was also found guilty of assaulting Murray and Patrick Clark. Paul Harris and Drennan were both cleared of the attack on Richard Boyle while the case against Claude Harris was found not proven in relation to that offence.

Despite the jury's plea for clemency, Lord Thomson showed no mercy and he sentenced the two brothers to death.

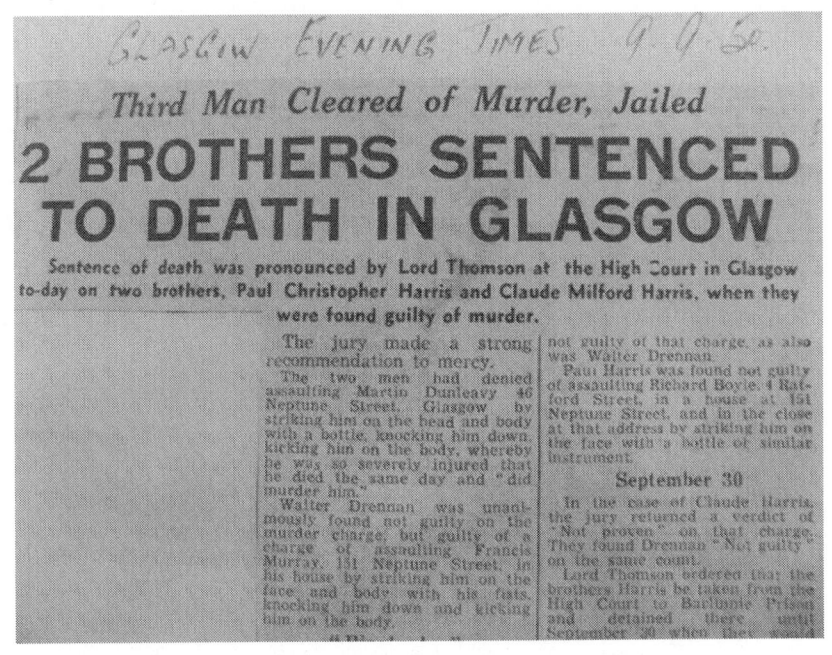

Glasgow Evening Times report on the death sentence

Incarcerated at Barlinnie, they were allowed to share the condemned cell, remaining as inseparable as ever. Both lodged legal appeals but Lord Cooper dismissed these on October 12.

He said that the case was not an easy one but added he was satisfied that there was enough evidence to warrant the conclusion that the fatal assault on Martin Dunleavy was committed by one or other of the two men and, although it was not clear who was responsible, they were acting together and were therefore equally guilty. A new date for execution was set for October 30.

During his time in the condemned cell, Paul Harris frequently talked about the night of the murder. He claimed six men were involved but only four were arrested. He refused to divulge the names of the other two.

Details of a meeting at Barlinnie between the brothers and their solicitor, Mr R.T. Cairns, reveal that this information only came to light after the trial evidence concluded.

Mr Cairns expressed surprised that after the jury had retired, he learned that there were six men involved after only four were mentioned in court.

At the prison meeting, he asked Paul Harris to let him have the names and addresses of the others. Harris suggested he ask Drennan who was less drunk at the time of the brawls. Harris claimed that most of the witnesses were related to or friends of Drennan and their evidence was lies 'made up' before the trial to shield Drennan.

Harris said he was unpopular in Neptune Street and did not expect anyone to speak in his favour. Before leaving the meeting, Cairns asked the brothers if they would care to think about it overnight and let him have a written statement. They again refused, repeating their assertion that he should speak to Drennan.

The Condemned Cell Occurrence Book also makes reference to six men being involved in the fight. A conversation between a warden and Paul Harris – while Claude Harris was asleep – was logged on September 25.

The officer wrote: 'Paul lay and talked about the night of the murder and recalled all that had happened. He said there were six men implicated although only four had been arrested.

'All through the conversation he kept bringing these two other men into it but would not divulge their names as it would only implicate them and he didn't want to do that.

'He says he never hit the murdered man with a bottle or weapon but admits kicking him and that his brother had nothing to do with it. He also admits hitting a person named Boyle over the head with a bottle.

'He said that Walter Drennan's sister went into the house after it had happened and saw a broken vase which Drennan had thrown during the fight and got rid of it. Also that she took a razor out of his pocket and hid it up the chimney.

'He also states that some of his [Drennan's] pals in Govan are beating up people who were at the trial and that it will be worse after the appeal no matter which way the appeal goes,' he added.

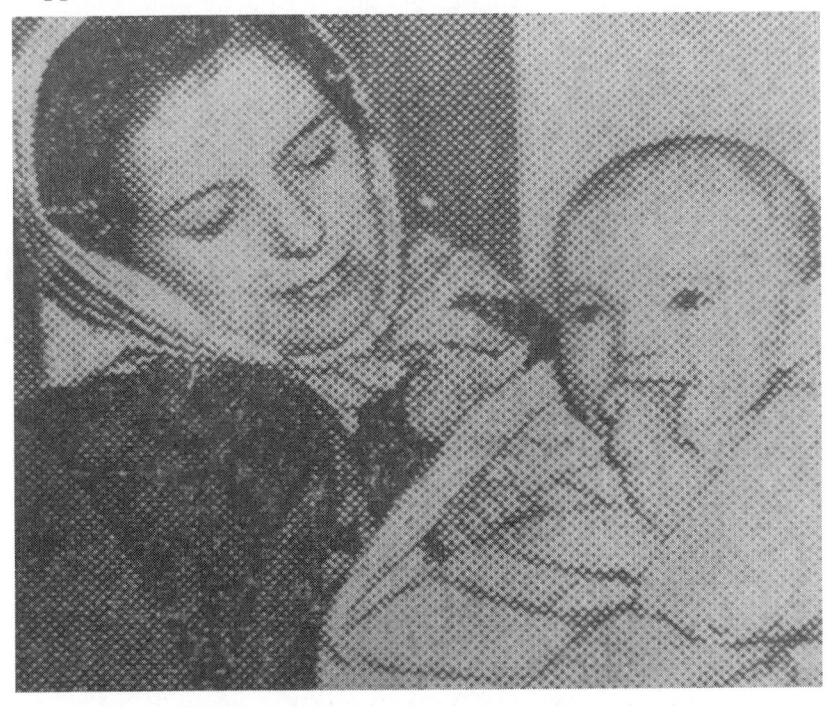

Ellen Harris and the couple's baby son

Paul Harris already had a good idea that he alone would face the consequences of that fateful night.

Prior to the trial, he wrote: 'When the trial comes up, I am expecting to see Claudie and Puggy [Drennan] getting off. As for yours truly, well I know they are out to do me. Somebody must suffer and they know I've got a record, so you can bet I'll be the fall guy.'

Harris, a lorry driver by trade, had a string of previous convictions that included housebreaking, theft, reset and malicious mischief. In 1940 he was sent to borstal for three years and between 1942 and 1948 he served four prison sentences ranging in length from six to 15 months.

His wife Ellen told him opinion on the Southside was that he would get a reprieve but he was not convinced. Dances were held to raise funds to pay for the legal costs of the brothers' appeal and a petition of 7000 signatures calling for clemency was sent to the Secretary of State for Scotland.

After careful consideration he responded, saying he 'regrets he is unable in either case to find sufficient grounds to justify him in advising interference with due course of law.' In other words there was to be no reprieve.

The Lord Provost delivered the news to the prisoners on October 27. His visit sparked an extraordinary turn of events that was to condemn Paul Harris but save his brother.

In an account held in the Barlinnie prison files, governor Joseph Mayo wrote: 'The Lord Provost arrived at the prison at 5.20pm and 10 minutes later told the Harris brothers the contents of the telegram to the effect that there was no reprieve. The chaplain visited the condemned cell as soon as he learned of the Lord Provost's visit.

'The Lord Provost was seated in his car ready to leave when the chaplain hurried from the condemned cell to tell me that Paul Harris wished to make a statement.'

The Lord Provost delayed his departure and the governor and chaplain, the Rev John Anderson, went straight to the condemned cell where Paul Harris said he would take full responsibility for

Dunleavy's death. His confession, along with a letter from his brother, was handed to the governor at 8.20pm.

In his letter, addressed to the Secretary of State, Harris wrote: I have now been told that no reprieve is to be given in my case and that I am to be put to death on Monday morning. I know that I shall soon meet my maker and with this in mind I solemnly and truly state that I alone was responsible for Dunleavy's death. I struck the blows. My brother Claude was not with me when it happened. He was out at the front part of the close when I was with Dunleavy. Claude did not see what happened.

'The plan of the close will show this. He was not with me at the time. This I swear to be the truth and I beg you to grant a reprieve to Claude. He never even saw me strike Dunleavy and he had no part in the assault.

'I state this solemnly as a man who is near the end and soon to meet his maker.'

The execution of Claude Harris was immediately postponed while the statement was considered.

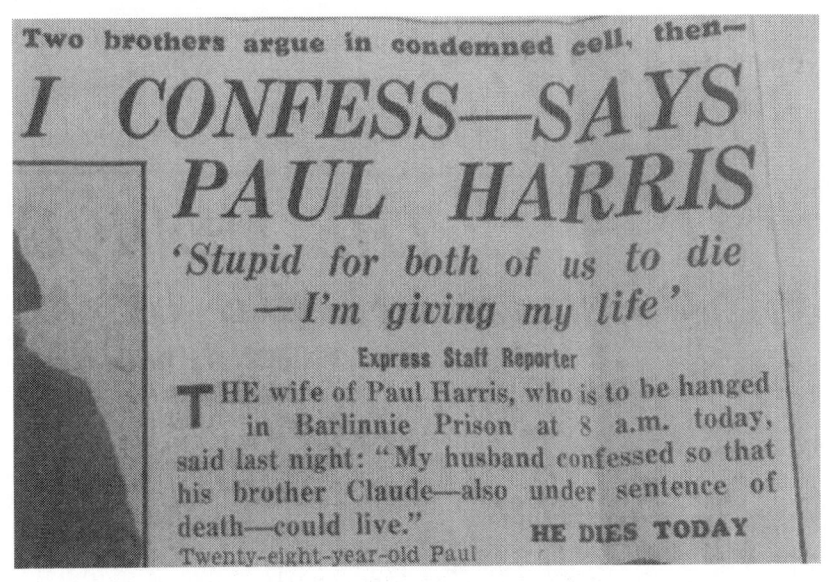

> **Two brothers argue in condemned cell, then—**
>
> # I CONFESS—SAYS PAUL HARRIS
>
> ## 'Stupid for both of us to die —I'm giving my life'
>
> **Express Staff Reporter**
>
> THE wife of Paul Harris, who is to be hanged in Barlinnie Prison at 8 a.m. today, said last night: "My husband confessed so that his brother Claude—also under sentence of death—could live." **HE DIES TODAY**
>
> Twenty-eight-year-old Paul

Newspaper report on the confession of Paul Harris

In a letter to his wife, Paul Harris subsequently wrote: 'It would have been stupid for both of us to die. A life has been taken and I'm giving mine in return. That should satisfy the world and let Claude go on living.'

There was considerable press interest in the story and Ellen Harris was keen to talk to reporters in a bid to save the necks of her husband and brother-in-law. Comments from some of the letters written by Paul Harris were quoted in newspapers, causing the prison authorities and government consternation.

Barlinnie governor Joseph Mayo took the unusual step of ordered his watching officers to pass details of all conversations in the condemned cell to him as soon as possible after it had been said. Marked 'urgent', the information was relayed straight to the Scottish Office.

Claude Harris was allowed to remain with his brother until midnight on the eve of the execution. As they parted, the two men shook hands and embraced. Claude was distraught.

'Ill be indebted to him until the day I die,' he said.

Another Harris brother, who visited the pair on the day before the execution, said: 'He [Claude] would rather have shared the blame with his brother. Paul behaved as if he was going to a party in the morning. He could always take his medicine.'

On the same day, Ellen made one last visit to her husband. He told her: 'What is the use of two of us going, after all I have done more fighting than him.'

Before she left him, he added: 'Make sure when our baby grows up he never takes drink.'

Prior to his execution, Paul Harris penned a letter to the governor thanking prison officers and the prison chaplain for the 'consideration' they had shown the pair during their stay at Barlinnie.

He later remarked: 'I am glad that Claudie and I have been together these past few weeks, it's made things a lot easier for both of us.'

With his brother detained elsewhere in the prison, Paul Harris rose at 6am on October 30, got dressed and took breakfast. At 8am he was led across the landing to the hanging chamber where Albert Pierrepoint, assisted by Stephen Wade, executed him. Outside the prison, a group of 15 people gathered to await news.

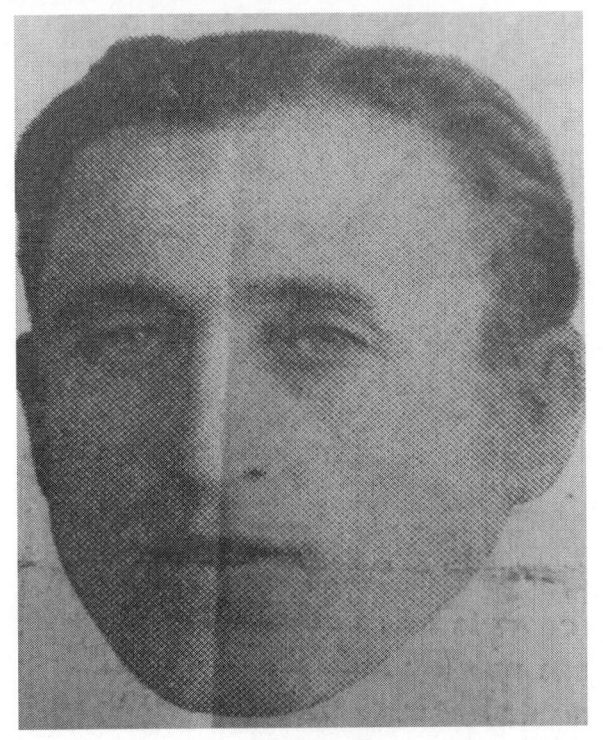

Claude Harris

Claude Harris was moved back into the condemned cell he had shared with his brother. A few days later word reached Barlinnie that he had been granted a reprieve and he was transferred to Perth Prison where he began a life sentence.

His wife Lilly Harris said: 'After Paul died, Claude used the same cell at his own request. He remained in it until the governor came to inform him of his reprieve. He wept with relief then began to realise he was alone.'

The inseparable Harrises had finally been separated.

*****

5. James Ronald Robertson

It was the early hours of Friday, July 28, 1950, 1.20am to be exact. Police Constable William Kevan arrived at the scene of a road accident. A woman's body lay on deserted Prospecthill Road, in Glasgow's Southside. Clearly there had been a fatal accident but PC Kevan believed there was more to it than initially met the eye.

A member of Glasgow's traffic department, he had been dispatched to the scene after taxi driver John Kennedy reported seeing a body lying on the quiet stretch of tarmac. On arrival, 45-year-old PC Kevan found the mangled remains of the victim, but as he pieced the clues together in his head he quickly came to the conclusion that things did not add up.

Officers at the scene of the 'accident'

'I thought the injuries too severe for an ordinary accident,' he said. 'I believed the body had been lain down.'

He noted too many inconsistencies for the incident to be a simple hit and run. There were two distinct sets of tyre marks around the body – one straight and the other curved. There were no skid marks, normally a good indication that a vehicle had braked heavily before hitting something, and no broken glass or other vehicle debris that one might expect to be found at the scene of a road accident.

While the victim had suffered serious injury, her lower legs – the point where a hit and run victim would normally come into contact with a car – were unscathed.

PC Kevan passed the matter to the local CID and Chief Inspector Dan McDougall, of the Southern Division, and his detective sergeant Murdoch McKenzie took up the case. All the evidence pointed to murder and the investigation began in earnest.

The first task was to identify the victim. She was carrying no identification, so officers enlisted the assistance of the Press and released information to the local papers appealing for anyone who might recognise the woman to come forward.

Shortly after the first editions of the Glasgow evening papers hit the streets, they received a call from a Mrs Johnston who was concerned that she had not seen her friend Catherine McCluskey since the previous night.

She told police that McCluskey had asked her to look after her baby as she had an important matter to take care of. After lying on a cold slab in the city mortuary for almost 14 hours, Catherine McCluskey was finally identified by her neighbour.

A single woman, 40-year-old Miss McCluskey lived in a room in a squalid tenement flat in Nicholson Street in the Gorbals with her two illegitimate children, a five-year-old boy and a three-month old boy. Both had different fathers.

Catherine McCluskey

After giving police a statement, Mrs Johnston revealed that Miss McCluskey had been planning to make a fresh start. She was going to settle down with a new man, the father of her baby. She told detectives the man, who she had not met, was a police officer by the name of Robertson.

Officers began sifting through the various Robertson's on the Glasgow force. Their job was made easier when they received a tip off suggesting they talk to PC James Robertson, who was rumoured to have been having marital problems and had been seeing a woman on the sly.

PC Robertson was duly called in but he denied any knowledge of Catherine McCluskey. Investigations, however, revealed that her lodgings were on his Gorbals beat and he had been out patrolling the streets at the time of the killing.

Detectives then interviewed Robertson's partner, PC Dugald Moffat, who confirmed that his colleague did indeed have a 'fancy woman'.

Moffat revealed that on quiet nights, Robertson would disappear off to spend time with her. On the night of July 28 he had done just that, returning to his beat at around 1am.

James Ronald Robertson

Police pulled in Robertson's dark blue Austin car for examination and on the underside found blood and fragments of hair, flesh and clothing.

The car, however, prompted even more questions. Officers discovered that it had originally been stolen from the centre of Glasgow and dumped on waste ground in West Campbell Street, close to Robertson's home.

Spotting it, he kept an eye on it for several days and after deciding it had been abandoned, claimed it for himself. Robertson put false plates on the car (the registration he picked officially belonged to a tractor kept on a farm in Aberdeenshire) and used it to take his family out for runs and even commuted to and from his work in it. He told colleagues he was looking after the car for a relative.

Officers linked him not only to the murder of Catherine McCluskey and the theft of the car, but also to a break in at Maine Motors in Cumberland Street where various items were stolen, including an electric clock, a wireless set, 14 car registration books, two tins of paint, a paint spray gun, bulbs, tyres, batteries and masking tape.

Robertson was known to have had a love of cars. At the age of 16, he had two motorcycles, one a powerful ex-police bike, and at 18 he acquired a small sports car. However, with a family to support on his modest police salary he could not afford to indulge his passion and when the opportunity to acquire the Austin came along, he took it.

Arrested for both murder and theft, Robertson denied all charges levied against him. He did finally admit to knowing Catherine McCluskey but was adamant he neither killed her nor was he having an affair with her.

The trial grabbed the attention of the people of Glasgow who were shocked to see a serving police officer being brought to book for such a brutal killing.

On November 6, 1950, the first day of Robertson's trial, under the headline 'Murder by Car - Trial Starts', the *Evening News* reported a packed courtroom.

'Over 100 people were still waiting in the street outside Glasgow High Court this afternoon when the trial of a 33-year-old Glasgow policeman, accused of killing a woman using a motor car as the murder weapon, was begun,' the report continued.

'The public gallery of the court was packed, all seats in the public section downstairs were filled and the doors to the court had to be closed.'

Shortly after 2pm, Robertson, six foot two inches tall and pale with a moustache, took his place in the dock.

He faced three charges, the first alleging that on April 23, 1950, he broken into Maine Motors and stole various items. The second charge alleged that on May 31, 1950, he stole a motorcar. The third and final charge accused him of assaulting and murdering Catherine McCluskey, striking her on the head with a rubber truncheon and driving the stolen car, then bearing a false registration number, over her.

In an attempt to establish a motive for murder, the prosecution focussed their inquiries on the nature of the relationship between Robertson and McCluskey.

An employee of the Department of Welfare told the court that McCluskey had on a number of occasions refused to reveal the identity of the father of her youngest child and as a result her weekly benefits were cut.

The prosecution suggested that this might have been the reason why Robertson and McCluskey argued on the night of her death. McCluskey, struggling to get by on a meagre state income, may have demanded money from the police officer and he refused. It was proposed that McCluskey may have been trying to blackmail Robertson and he could no longer take it.

Stepping on to the stand to give evidence in his defence, Robertson said that he met McCluskey the previous year in the course of his duties when he was called to her home to deal with a disturbance. He admitted that he had met her on a few occasions since then and agreed that they were on friendly terms.

Under cross-examination, he denied that he was having an affair with her or that he was the father of her baby.

On the night of Thursday, July 27, 1950, McCluskey had asked to meet up with him and, slipping away from his beat, they went for a drive in his car. Robertson claimed she had asked him to take her to the village of Neilston in Renfrewshire. He refused, telling her it was too far away and the journey would take him away from his beat for too long.

An argument ensued and Robertson said that as they drove along Prospecthill Road, McCluskey became hysterical and demanded to get out of the car.

Robertson duly pulled over and after McCluskey got out, he drove off. However, he told the court he promptly had a change of heart, saying he felt he could not leave her alone on the road, far from home during the early hours of the morning.

Robertson claimed he reversed the vehicle back along the road towards her but when he heard a dull thud he stopped and got out to investigate. He saw McCluskey under the vehicle and quickly came to the conclusion that she was dead.

He told the court that her clothing was entangled with the prop shaft and in an attempt to free the vehicle he had driven it back and forth several times. Unsure of what to do next, he drove off.

Robertson parked the vehicle in the Gorbals and returned to his beat, meeting up with PC Moffat. Before ending his shift, he penned an entry in the beat journal relating to the accident.

It read: 'At 12.50am today, a woman was knocked down and fatally injured in Prospecthill Road near Aitkenhead Road. The motor car, believed to be a small blue Austin, maybe 10hp, was driven by a man wearing a light fawn Burberry coat. The car did not stop and was last seen driving citywards on Aitkenhead Road.'

During the trial the jury was led out to a yard behind the courthouse where its members were shown the car, the alleged murder weapon. It had been hoisted on to its side so they could examine the underside of the chassis. Crucially, they were able to see the that the prop shaft was entirely enclosed, casting more than a little doubt over Robertson's claim that McCluskey's dress and jacket had become caught in it.

The trial also heard expert medical evidence that revealed the extent of the dead woman's injuries. The Chief Medical Officer of Glasgow Police, Dr James Imrie, said her jaw was broken in three separate places, her left ear had been virtually torn off and there were fractures to her nose, breast bone, pelvis and ribs.

A second physician, Dr Andrew Allison, said that McCluskey's injuries were 'more gross than he had ever met in an accident with a private car'.

The two men were convinced that McCluskey had been struck on the head before being placed on the road. They believed the blow had rendered her unconscious and that the fatal injuries resulted from her being run over.

Unconvinced by Robertson's claim he had accidentally reversed over Catherine McCluskey, the jury found him guilty of murder by a majority after deliberating for a little over an hour. They also convicted him on the two theft charges.

Donning a black cap at the end of the weeklong trial, Lord Justice Keith had the dubious distinction of sentencing a serving police officer to death. The execution was scheduled for December 4.

Outside the court a large crowd had gathered for the verdict and an army of police officers was mustered to hold the throng back. As Robertson left the building to board the van to Barlinnie, where he would spend the remainder of his days, he was shielded from view by constables who held up sheets of tarpaulin.

Brought up in Clydebank, Robertson worked with engines from an early age, starting his first job at Beardmore's before moving to Singer and then Rolls Royce where he was an inspector of aircraft engines.

Married with two young children, he was described as a devoted husband and father. He did not smoke or drink and when he was not working he spent his time with his family.

He joined the police force in November 1945 and was assigned a beat in the Gorbals, a largely residential area of the city where hundreds lived in rundown four-storey tenement blocks. It was a grim neighbourhood where poverty and crime were rife and opportunities were few and far between.

Despite his air of respectability – the perfect family man – Robertson was said to have harboured a darker side, one of illicit affairs conducted behind the back of his doting wife. After his trial, the *Daily Express* reported that on his beat he boasted to colleagues of dates with women. Catherine McCluskey was one of these women.

Anecdotal evidence suggested he met her in the street late one night. She approached him looking to change coins to feed her gas meter. He obliged and, as it was a cold, wet night, she invited him in for a warming cup of tea. Robertson became a regular visitor to her home.

James Ronald Robertson and his family

In Barlinnie, Robertson shared the condemned cell with Matthew Graham, a fellow murderer who stabbed a woman to death in Clydebank. Extracts from the Condemned Cell Occurrence Book reveal Robertson had a tendency to discuss escape methods with Graham and were he to break free he would head for Edinburgh. There is no evidence to suggest he ever attempted to enact his plans and make a bid for freedom from the legendary stronghold.

The former police officer's appeal failed and the Secretary of State for Scotland rejected a petition seeking a reprieve.

Despite lurid Press speculation about his private life, Robertson remained in regular contact with his wife Janette who, by this stage, had moved from the former family home in Craigmuir Road, Glasgow, to the Scottish Borders.

The convicted cop continued to protest his innocence, branding newspaper coverage of his trial as lies, and blamed his predicament on the stolen Austin.

In a letter to Janette, penned on December 13, he wrote: 'I have all sorts of feelings about it all and it makes my heart bleed to think so many things have gone so far wrong with me, all on account of an old motor car. I've thought it out hundreds of ways and I'm convinced that no matter what angle I adopted and what story I put forward, the result would have been the same.'

Ironically, legal experts believe Robertson may have escaped the hangman's noose had he admitted to having an affair with McCluskey. His lawyer Laurence Dowdall later said: 'The extraordinary thing about it was that if he had told the truth in the witness box he would never have been convicted of murder.

'His wife knew that he had been conducting this liaison but he said he was not going to let her down in public. If he had told the truth and admitted he had this illicit liaison with this woman McCluskey then he would have got off.'

James Ronald Robertson with his wife and children

Dowdall believes that Robertson's continued assertion in court that McCluskey was no more than a 'casual acquaintance' was his downfall and resulted in the jury viewing him as a cold-blooded killer rather than a man caught in a tortuous relationship between his loving wife and mistress.

'Had the jury known of the relationship they might have viewed the killing in a different, more sympathetic light,' Dowdall added. 'There could have been a lesser charge or sentence.'

Robertson, however, continued to blame the car. On the eve of his execution, he wrote again to his wife.

'I am praying for your Mum too that she might forgive and forget my car episode but she knows that was my worst mistake, the running around in the stolen car.'

If Robertson is to be believed, his lifelong passion for cars brought about his demise. The High Court, however, ruled that he used his beloved motor vehicle as a murder weapon to coldly kill a 'casual acquaintance'. On December 16, 1950, he paid the ultimate price.

At 8am, he made the short walk from the condemned cell to the gallows where Albert Pierrepoint and his assistant Stephen Wade were waiting. A minute later Robertson, the only serving police officer to be executed in Britain in the 20th century, was dead.

*****

6. James Smith

Outwardly at least, James Smith was a dapper young man. When he went out dancing of a night he was always smartly dressed, wearing a pressed shirt, tie and stylish two-piece suit. He took a great deal of pride in his appearance, combing back his black hair, the height of fashion for a young man in those days. But he didn't go for the girls or the dancing. He went for the fighting and if there was ever any trouble you could bet your last shilling he was at the heart of it.

The 20-year-old Springburn lad was a notorious troublemaker with a string of previous convictions for truancy, theft, breach of the peace and assault. On the night of November 16, 1951, he would add murder to this list.

The Ancient Order of Hibernians Hall in Royston Road was hosting a dance to raise money for old age pensioners. It was due to be a busy one; dances in Glasgow in the 1950s and 60s were always popular and, as was unfortunately usually the case, there was bound to be trouble. Fuelled by heavy drinking and simmering rivalry, fighting was all part of a night out in Glasgow for some. But the scraps normally fizzled out when those involved were ejected on to the street, allowing the revellers to dance on into the early hours.

Dressed to impress, Smith left home in Wallacewell Road, where he lived with his parents, and met up with friends. They drank beer and whisky in a couple of pubs before heading to the hall, located in an area known as The Garngad. It was a Catholic stronghold in a part of the city where there was a long tradition of Sectarianism that frequently erupted on the streets with fights between Catholics and Protestants common.

Smith arrived at the hall at around 9.45pm with four mates. However before they had even entered the building, there was trouble at the door. Two older men, Martin Malone and his friend William Loudon, had arrived some 15 minutes earlier. In the scuffle, Loudon punched one of Smith's pals, Robert McKenna, in the face causing his nose to bleed.

Smith stepped in, dragging McKenna into the ladies cloakroom. In the meantime, Malone and Loudon proceeded upstairs to the dance floor where Malone found his wife, Mary, whom he had arranged to meet earlier in the night. Loudon hooked up with a woman.

James Smith

Ten minutes later, Smith headed up to the dancing. By this stage, however, he was armed with a dagger which he later claimed his friend Joseph O'Rourke had slipped into his pocket following the altercation at the door.

Keen to avenge his injured friend, Smith crossed the dance floor, heading straight for Loudon. He grabbed the man's shoulder and, without warning, plunged the knife in below the ribs.

Loudon fell to the floor, writhing in agony. Witnesses testified that Malone, spotting the commotion, immediately left his wife and went to his friend's assistance. He attempted to pick Loudon up but swiftly Smith turned on him.

In the ensuing fight, Malone was stabbed twice, once on the lower jaw and the second time on the left side of his body, the blade driving deep into his lung.

Smith threw his dagger away but as he attempted to flee the scene he was caught and held by one of the dance hall staff.

A policeman searched him and, after the officer found no weapons on him, he was released, free to go despite the hubbub on the dance floor. It is likely, however, that at this stage the true horror of what had happened had not yet become fully apparent.

Smith raced across the crowded dance floor towards the main entrance. However, as he headed down the stairs, Mary Malone, who instantly recognised him as her husband's attacker, blocked his path. He turned on his heels and bounded back up the stairs where, after a brief tussle with the officer who had earlier searched him, he escaped through an emergency exit.

The *Evening Citizen* reported that following the stabbings police surrounded the hall and allowed none of the 300 people in attendance to leave until they had completed their inquiries, which continued until 3am. As word of the incident spread and as officers streamed into the hall, large crowds of onlookers gathered in the street outside.

With his lung punctured, Malone died at the scene. His friend was taken by ambulance to Glasgow Royal Infirmary where he underwent emergency surgery. Loudon spent six days in hospital recovering from the attack before being allowed home.

Despite the fatal stabbing, the dance continued for sometime, until police brought it to an end. One of the officers who attended, Sergeant Peter Peebles, later told the High Court: 'While Malone lay dying on the floor the band still played and one or two couples were still trying to dance.'

It had, however, been a night peppered with sporadic outbursts of violence – earlier four men were thrown out for fighting – so they may have been forgiven for thinking this was just another dust-up.

However, it was far from that. Peebles' colleague Constable Denis Joyce recalled entered the hall with another officer. He saw Malone lying on the floor at the far end of the room, being attended to by an ambulance man.

'There was a sort of trail of blood from the middle of the dance floor – there were spots of blood, a large patch of blood, and another patch beside the dead man's head.'

This suggests that Malone, assisted by others, had attempted to drag himself off the floor.

Officers soon found the murder weapon and, after taking dozens of witness statements, detectives were ready to make an arrest. At 4.30am, after a lengthy search, they found Smith, asleep in bed, at a relative's house in the Blackhill district of the city.

Still dressed in his smart suit and with his hair slicked back, Smith appeared in the dock at the Glasgow Northern Police Court where he was charged with the murder of 35-year-old shipyard worker Martin Malone and the assault to severe injury on his 38-year-old friend William Loudon.

The *Evening News* reported: 'He stood stiffly, his white features a striking contrast to his jet-black, sleekly brushed hair'.

Smith denied the charges brought against him and, on February 26, 1952, the case went to trial at the city's High Court. Giving evidence in his own defence, Smith claimed that he thought Loudon might be armed and went over to call his bluff.

'I said: "What's all this about?",' Smith told the jury.

'Loudon seemed to make a lunge at me. I lost my head, struck him with the knife.

'He fell. I stood dazed with the knife in my hand. I heard footsteps at my back, got a kick in the leg, turned and saw Malone running at me.

'He seemed to have what looked like a small, black British Army bayonet in his hand. He didn't seem able to stop. I grabbed him and we both fell on the slippery dance floor.'

Smith was asked: 'At that time did you have the dagger in your hand?'

'Yes, sir,' he replied.

'Were you conscious of doing anything to Malone?'

'No.'

Smith claimed that Malone fell on top of him, and he tried to get him off. Malone, he said, must have received his two stab wounds by accident as they fell together, both holding knives.

The judge, Lord Cooper, asked: 'Do you say you do not know which weapon it was that caused injury to Malone's body – whether it was your dagger or the weapon which you say he was carrying?'

Smith replied: 'Yes.'

After the stabbing, Smith claimed that he felt dazed.

'Someone picked me up and put me on a seat. I went out through the back door.'

Unfortunately for Smith, there were no witnesses to support his version of events and no one came forward to say they had seen Malone with a knife in his hand.

There was some controversy at the trial after a second knife, handed to police on the day after the murder, was revealed. It had been found under a seat in the hall but was not produced in court until after Smith had lodged a special plea of self-defence.

Smith's lawyer described it as 'disgraceful' that nothing was done to test the weapon for blood or fingerprints.

In his address to the jury, Lord Cooper said: 'Although Smith stated he was threatened by Loudon and later attacked by Malone with a weapon in his hand, Smith was unmarked. One of his assailants was removed to the Royal Infirmary and operated upon; the other was dead. Smith made his escape from the hall and went home to bed.'

Lord Cooper said that if Smith's claim that he acted in self-defence was not accepted, the jury might nevertheless find that there was an element of provocation.

'This might induce you to regard the crime in relation to Malone as one not of murder but of culpable homicide.'

The jury, however, was not convinced it was self-defence and took 95 minutes to unanimously convict Smith of the murder of Malone and the attack on Loudon.

Lord Cooper sentenced Smith to death by hanging and he was taken from the court to the condemned cell at Barlinnie Prison.

Smith had what was described in subsequent psychological reports as a 'fairly normal' childhood but at the age of 13, he was sent to St Mary's Approved School in Glasgow following persistent truancy. He remained there for two years.

In the years that followed he racked up a significant criminal record for one so young and was convicted on charges of theft, breach of the peace and assault.

James Smith being led from the High Court in Glasgow

Glasgow Chief Constable Malcolm McCulloch said that most of Smith's associates were known thieves, adding: 'Very little can be said in his favour'.

Smith, who worked briefly as a labourer and spent 130 days in the army before being discharged as 'permanently unfit' for any form of military service, blamed his criminal career on the influence of delinquent and criminal youth he encountered at St Mary's.

Even his time at Barlinnie was not without incident. While on remand awaiting trial, Smith attacked a prison officer. After shouting and swearing following a prison visit, an agitated Smith was placed in a cell by the reception area to cool off. However, upon his release, he kicked the officer with full force in the face. The officer sustained a cut on the bridge of his nose that required stitches.

The prisoner's governor described him as a 'dull, morose man with a generally unpleasant manner and with singularly few interests'.

In prison, he was said to frequently spit on the floor and had the eating habits of 'an animal'.

Following his conviction Press reports described Smith as both an 'arrogant' and 'bitter' young man. People who knew him said after his brief stint in the army he became 'very hard and bitter'.

One unnamed man, who claimed to know the family and was quoted in the *Daily Mail* on March 26, said: 'He never went about with girls. Yet he often went to dances and when there was trouble there, James was in the thick of it. He loved a fight.

'He was completely contained within himself. He became truculent, even belligerent and arrogant and could never be corrected on any point.'

However, there was much support for him within his local community, few believing he was capable of murder. Upon his conviction, hundreds travelled down from The Garngad and gathered outside the High Court to protest at the sentence delivered upon him.

Smith's legal team immediately lodged an appeal. His lawyer argued that there had been a miscarriage of justice, as the second dagger found in the hall had not been produced in evidence.

The police argued that they had not initially put it forward as they had not felt it relevant to the case. Knives, daggers and bayonets were frequently found in dance halls following trouble. It was common practice for those in possession of such weapons to either discard or try to hide them when the police arrived, whether or not they were involved.

After four days of legal debate, the three appeal court judges ruled that the second knife was not central to the conviction since there was no evidence, even circumstantial, that it was Malone's knife. The appeal was dismissed on March 25 and a plea for clemency was rejected.

The date of execution was set and arrangements were made to bring Albert Pierrepoint and his tools of the trade to Barlinnie.

On the eve of his death, Smith wrote a letter to Malone's widow Mary expressing his sorrow that she had lost her husband, adding: 'I hope you will forgive me for it as I never tried to kill him.'

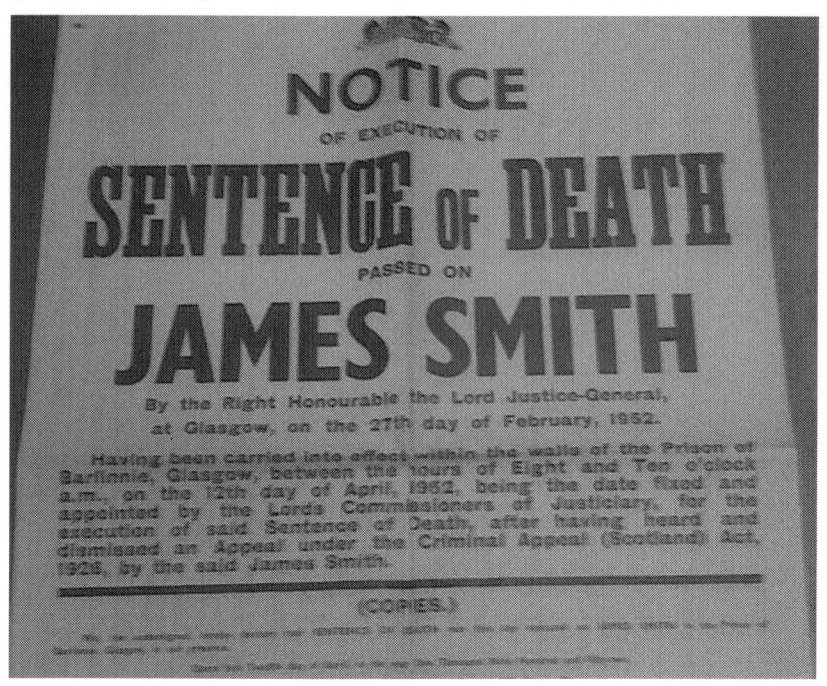

James Smith Notice of Execution of Sentence of Death

The letter was never sent and, protesting his innocence to the end, Smith took his last steps across the floor to the hanging cell where, at 8.01am on April 12, he was executed.

*****

7. Patrick Gallacher Deveney

Jeanie Deveney knew her husband was going to kill her. She could see it in his eyes.

Friend and neighbour Georgina Wilson told her not to be so stupid. 'You read too many crime magazines,' she said. But when Mrs Wilson called at the Deveney house later the same day to pick up a book, she rattled the letterbox and no one answered. Little did she know that inside Jeanie Deveney lay dead.

She and her husband Patrick, a former soldier, were locked in an unhappy marriage. They wed on January 14, 1937. Deveney was on leave from the army when they met and within a week they were husband and wife.

Deveney was a fresh faced young man, 5ft 8ins tall with blue eyes and light brown hair. During his tours of duty, he picked up numerous tattoos. These included a large crucifix on his back, a Union Jack with the words 'Death or Glory' on his forearm, a horse's head, a female figure and swallows on the back of both hands.

The couple shared a cramped tenement flat in Blackburn Street with their five children, three boys and two girls. It was not a happy home. They argued frequently – most of the time about money and Deveney's unemployed – and split up on numerous occasions. But every time, she returned to her man.

Her mother, Mrs Mary Todd, told how after yet another spat, Jeanie turned up at her home claiming he had threatened to kill her. When Mrs Todd asked her daughter what made her think that, Jeanie replied: 'It's his eyes. I don't know what's the matter with his eyes.'

Mrs Todd revealed that on the weekend before her death, her 36-year-old daughter was adamant she was going to leave her husband, this time for good.

At 8pm on the Saturday, Mrs Todd, who spent the day looking after two of her grandchildren, set off to return the youngsters to their mother. As she entered the common close in Blackburn Street and started going up the stairs, her daughter came running down and ordered her back.

She asked why and Jeanie Deveney screamed that her husband was after her and he had thrown two bottles of milk at her.

Describing her daughter as upset and distressed, Mrs Todd took her and the children home with her. She persuaded her daughter to spend both Saturday and Sunday night at her house in Middlesex Street.

On Sunday, her daughter, who worked as a cleaner at a gent's outfitters in the city's Argyle Street to make ends meet, said she planned to leave her husband. She wanted to keep the children and the house, but she wanted him out of her life.

On Monday morning Mrs Deveney, set off for work as normal but returned in the afternoon saying she had given up her job because her husband had been waiting for her outside the shop. This was something he had apparently been doing for a number of weeks.

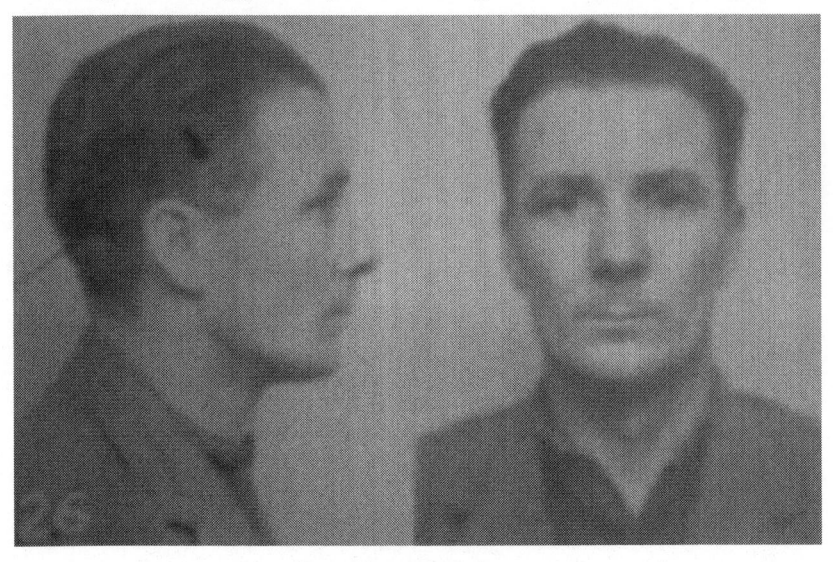

Patrick Deveney

'Jeanie said that she would live with him for another week,' Mrs Todd recalled. 'He had told her that he would go away at the end of the week and leave her in peace.

'She said he had also told her that if she did not go back, he would kill her. She was in a very distressed condition and was very upset.'

Mother and daughter talked matters through and Mrs Todd told her: 'Don't stay there because something is sure to happen.'

Despite this warning, Jeanie Deveney returned to the unsettled family home, accompanied by her 31-year-old brother George. Patrick Deveney was there when they arrived but once she was settled her brother left.

On Tuesday evening, 44-year-old Patrick Deveney turned up at his brother Hugh's home in Greenock. With him was his five-year-old daughter Betty.

Hugh Deveney, who had just returned home from work, said: 'He seemed to be looking through me. He looked vacant. When I asked him if anything was wrong, he just mumbled and said he wanted to go to the police.'

A second brother, Daniel, joined them and they made their way through the streets to Greenock Police Station.

Daniel said: 'I definitely did not think he was in his right mind. I thought he was crazy.'

At the police station, Patrick Deveney told officers that there was 'something wrong' with his wife, adding that she was in the family home in Blackburn Street. He handed over the house door key.

Officers decided further enquiries were in order before they visited the house. George Todd received a visit from two policemen that same evening and he accompanied them to Plantation Police Office.

They asked him if he knew where his sister was and after about 15 minutes Todd accompanied them to her house.

The policemen had to force entry to the property as the door was locked. Todd entered the kitchen and switched on the light.

He said: 'First thing I saw was bedclothes all in a pile on the floor. They were heaped between the bed and the fireplace.

'There was a pool of blood in front of the sink. There was also a small nailbrush there and on the right of that, in front of the coal bunker there was a coal hammer.'

Todd said he saw a set of dentures lying in the pool of blood.

'I looked down at the heap of bedclothes and I saw a hand sticking out.'

The two officers investigated further and to their horror discovered that Jeanie Deveney, dressed in outdoor clothes and an overcoat, was dead. She had been beaten on the head with the coal hammer and strangled with a tie.

Police did not have to look far for a suspect. He was already in Greenock Police Station. Patrick Deveney was questioned and then charged with the murder of his wife. When they searched him, they found a large bloodstain on the left sleeve of his shirt and spots of blood on his trousers and shoes.

In May 1952, Deveney appeared in the dock at the High Court in Glasgow, charged with assaulting his wife, striking her on the head with a hammer and strangling her with a necktie, and murdering her.

The court heard evidence of the unhappy marriage from Mrs Todd and the threats made by Deveney towards his wife.

Neighbour and friend Georgina Wilson, who lived in the flat immediately below the Deveney home, told the court that on the Tuesday morning Jeanie Deveney visited her and claimed her husband had threatened to 'cut her in pieces'.

Mrs Wilson added: 'I told her she had been reading too many crime magazines.'

At 5pm Mrs Wilson called at the Deveney house. She rattled the letterbox but there was no answer.

Witnesses gave evidence on the movements of Deveney and his wife on the day of the killingr. One saw Deveney return home at 2pm and another witnessed Mrs Deveney leave the flat at 2.30pm. A third witness saw Mrs Deveney walking in the direction of her home at

2.50pm. A fourth testified that Deveney returned home just after 3pm and left again at 3.15pm.

Police Constable Neil Smith told the court that on the Monday Deveney visited Plantation Police Station and lodged a complaint against George Todd, claiming he had broken into the house and assaulted him. However, upon further investigation it was accepted that Todd had simply walked into the house, with his sister, and brushed past Deveney.

Advocate-depute Mr D.M. Campbell said: 'We do not know exactly what happened between these two but it is not an unreasonable inference that some sort of struggle occurred.

'There was blood near the sink. There was a smear of blood on the wallpaper. And the woman's body was lying between the fireplace and bed, covered with a heap of bedclothes. The murder took place sometime between 2pm and 4pm.'

Although Mrs Deveney was struck on the head with a hammer, the cause of death was strangulation.

A roll of bloodstained linoleum lifted from the kitchen floor was among the Crown productions displayed in court.

The defence claimed that Deveney had a 'psychopathic personality' and that he suffered regular blackouts and was a heavy consumer of aspirin. His brother Hugh told the court that he suffered severe headaches after returning from army service in Palestine in 1937 and 'took aspirins by he handful', sometimes as many as 100 a day.

Expert defence witness, psychiatrist Dr William Blythe, said that he had examined the accused and come to the conclusion that he was sane and of normal intelligence.

However, he described Deveney's judgement as 'faulty' and said he was struck by the man's 'abnormal' affection for his daughter Betty and his relative indifference to the other members of his family. The doctor said he did not believe this was the behaviour of a normal man.

Dr Blythe revealed that Deveney told him he was quite willing to hang provided the authorities gave him a guarantee that Betty, the second youngest of his five children, would be looked after.

Evidence concluded, Lord Keith instructed the jury: 'You have to distinguish between such things as quick temper, anti-social tendencies and lack of control, things that we all suffer from in greater or lesser degree.'

'We all suffer from absent-mindedness at times in a minor degree. You've got to consider whether these qualities are really evidences of mental disease.

'If you think it was the act of a man suffering from mental disease, then you would return a verdict of culpable homicide. If you don't think it's such an act, then you must not shrink from returning a verdict of murder,' he added.

On May 8, after 40 minutes of deliberation, the jury of eight men and seven women returned to the courtroom and delivered a unanimous verdict of guilty to the charge of murder.

Deveney was sentenced to death and did not appeal.

Born in Wishaw in 1908 Deveney served as a soldier and later worked as a labourer. He was discharged from the army before the end of the Second World War after displaying signs of a 'psychopathic' personality.

He had a number of previous convictions. In his late teens, he was sent to borstal for three years after he was caught trying to break into a house. He later served three short sentences in Greenock Prison for theft.

Although waiving his right to appeal, Deveney did petition the Secretary of State for a reprieve but it was done with little optimism or enthusiasm.

Extracts from the Condemned Cell Occurrence Book reveal that Deveney read and played dominoes while he awaited execution.

He told his guards he did not care whether he was hanged or sentenced to life imprisonment, but claimed if he got life and could not settle down he would probably commit suicide.

At 8am on May 29, Deveney stepped out of the condemned cell and into the execution chamber where Albert Pierrepoint and his assistant Stephen Wade sent him to the grave. It was rather fitting that having despatched his wife with a noose fashioned from his necktie, Deveney ended his life in such a similar way.

With both mother and father dead, the Deveney children, whose ages ranged from four to 12, were placed in care and, according to family members, experienced a traumatic and stigmatised childhood.

His beloved daughter Betty developed an alcohol problem and died aged 36.

*****

8. George Francis Shaw

Michael Connelly – affectionately known as Old Mick – was an unlikely murder victim. For over three decades the retired miner lived a frugal existence in a tumbledown hut he constructed from discarded materials on farmland in Lanarkshire. He was reclusive, kept himself to himself, and was regarded by others as something of a hermit, surviving on the margins of society with neither friends nor enemies. He had few material possessions beyond the clothes he stood up in and little money. He scratched a living doing odd jobs on a local farm during harvest time and received a small weekly pension.

The hut Connelly called home was tiny. Constructed from wood, corrugated iron sheets and tarpaulin, it measured just four feet in height and eight feet in length. The main room was barely large enough for the old mattress he slept upon.

Once or twice a week he walked into the nearby town of Lanark to collect his pension and buy groceries. The rest of his time he spent alone, his isolation occasionally interrupted by friendly locals who would drop in to check on him or deliver parcels of food or paraffin for his stove.

In August 1952, his lonely and uncomplicated life came to a brutal end. Connelly, who was 79 at the time and walked with a limp and a stick, was alone in his hut in the corner of a field on Huntlygate Farm, near Lanark, when he was beaten to death with an iron bar, a brick and a lemonade bottle. The old man's battered body was found lying on his bed on August 24 by two young men who stopped by the hut to see how he was. To their horror, they saw broken glass on the bed and blood spattered on the bedposts and floor. Connelly's boots were off and his trouser pockets had been slit, torn or ripped open. The police were immediately alerted and a murder hunt was launched.

Officers began by piecing together the victim's last known movements, not an easy task when dealing with someone who lived such an isolated existence. They discovered that Connelly, who was believed to have originally come from Ireland and had moved down to Lanark from Bathgate in West Lothian, had drawn his pension as normal from the local Post Office on August 15. Two days later, he was in town shopping and was seen by witnesses returning home with bags of groceries.

Although he seldom visited the town, he was a well-known local character. After collecting his money, he purchased his provisions and left. He never lingered long and did not visit the local public houses, hotel bars or cafes.

Witnesses said Connelly 'kept himself to himself and did not take often to people'. There was no evidence to suggest he had any enemies and there was nothing in his conduct to give reason for an attack on him.

Inquiries then focussed on whether the crime had been a robbery that went horrifically wrong. Anecdotal evidence drawn from members of the community suggested Connelly hoarded cash within the old shack. The hut was carefully taken apart by officers but other than a 1942 farthing, no money was found. The only other possessions uncovered were a bible, a pipe, a candleholder, two battered spectacle cases, a razor, a rabbit snare and a tool bag.

Within the hut, officers found a bloodstained towel. Around 250 yards away, they discovered a footprint and a bloodstained piece of cloth and a little further out, at 300 yards, they found a blue coat, also heavily stained with blood, dumped in long grass.

Inquiries continued and a witness came forward to report that on August 17 he had seen the old man in the company of another man who was described as wearing 'battle dress'. Another witness saw this suspect and another man in the area of the hut on the same date.

During the investigation farm labourers George Francis Shaw (25) and George Dunn (22) were interviewed as part of routine police inquiries and initially neither were suspected of having any involvement in the crime.

However, as the clues came together, police decided the pair warranted further examination. Both men lived on a local farm where officers found a battledress blouse belonging to Dunn. It had a bloodstain on it.

It also came to light that Shaw had lost his job two weeks earlier, yet managed to pay Mrs Sybil Cairns, the mother of his three children, £2 towards their upkeep on August 17.

George Francis Shaw

Witnesses came forward to say that they had seen the pair on the afternoon and evening of August 17 spending money 'freely' in a hotel bar in Kirkfieldbank, a few miles from Lanark. The two men were said to have been buying food and drink with a roll of new £1 notes.

Born in County Mayo in Ireland, the second eldest of six sons and two daughters, Shaw attended school until he was 14. Aged 15, he moved to Scotland and worked with potato squads in Ayrshire and Lanarkshire. After a brief period as a trainee miner with the National Coal Board in Fife, he enlisted in the Royal Scots in 1945 and served in the regiment for five years before transferring to the King's Own Scottish Borderers. However, he was discharged in March 1950 for misconduct and returned to farm work. His military conduct was described as 'indifferent'.

He was known to police, both in his home country and in Scotland. In 1942 he was convicted in Ireland of his involvement in the theft of a purse containing £1 and in 1949 he added an assault conviction to his record following an incident in Stranraer, a busy port on the south west coast of Scotland.

Although the evidence gathered was entirely circumstantial, police decided they had enough to arrest Shaw and Dunn. Ironically, when the two men were taken into custody, both were wearing socks that had originally belonged to Connelly. Shaw said he acquired the socks innocently and denied being with Dunn on August 17.

When interviewed by officers, Shaw claimed he did not know of Connelly or his hut. He admitted that he and his friend Dunn had met an old man near Huntlygate Farm, but he did not know who the man was and had not spoken with him.

Dunn, however, cracked early on and admitted he did know Connelly and told police they were both at the hut.

In his statement he said: 'I was out at the hut with Frank Shaw but I didn't touch the old man. It was Shaw who killed him and he threw the iron bar and bit of bottle amongst the grass, then he washed his hands in the burn and used a towel he got in the hut. Frank had on the blue coat and it was all blood and he hid it in the grass.'

During a week of intense questioning, Shaw refused to confess to the murder.

On November 22, 1952, the pair appeared in the dock at the High Court in Glasgow. They were charged with assaulting Michael Connelly, striking him on the hands, face and head with a brick, an iron bar and a bottle, robbing him of two pairs of socks and an unknown amount of money, and murdering him.

Both men denied the charge and their trial began on December 2, 1952.

The Crown claimed that both Shaw and Dunn were seen in the area of the hut on August 17 and linked both a footprint found 250 yards from the shack and the bloodstained army-style coat to Shaw.

Covering the proceedings, the *Daily Express* described Shaw as a 'burly' man who 'smiled during most of his week-long trial for murder'.

For his part, Shaw lodged a defence of alibi, claiming he was elsewhere at the time of the murder while Dunn was described by his lawyer as a 'feeble minded person'. Medical evidence suggested he had the mental age of an eight-year-old child.

The court heard that Connelly's skull was fractured in the attack and there were injuries to his brain.

A bread salesman indicating that Connelly did indeed have enough money tucked away in his hut to pay for his own funeral also gave evidence.

Presiding over the trial, Lord Curmont said as he opened his summing up: 'When old Michael Connelly was found in his hut on August 24 it did not take long to determine that he had been murdered.

'Some murderer struck those vicious, brutal blows.'

Even though the evidence led by the Crown was entirely circumstantial, on December 9 the jury found Shaw guilty of murder and convicted Dunn of culpable homicide by a majority of 11 to three.

Dunn was sent to the Carstairs Institution for Mental Defectives (now the State Hospital at Carstairs) and Shaw was sentenced to death.

He was taken to Barlinnie where he was incarcerated within the condemned cell. There he occupied his time reading and playing cards.

With the gallows looming large over what remained of his life, Shaw protested his innocence in letters to family and friends and lodged an appeal against conviction on December 29.

In a letter to his father, he sounded less than optimistic about his chances of gaining a reprieve. He wrote: 'I am not too bad. I am building no hopes. I will just wait and see what will happen. The QC said I have a good chance both ways.'

To his girlfriend Sybil Cairns, he wrote: 'I might get off and I might not. It all depends on the judges. If they think my style suits, then I am alright.'

Clearly Shaw's style did not suit. After a hearing in early January 1953, his appeal was rejected and the original conviction was upheld.

The *Evening Citizen* reported: 'Before the judges entered the court, Shaw laughed and joked with the wardens.

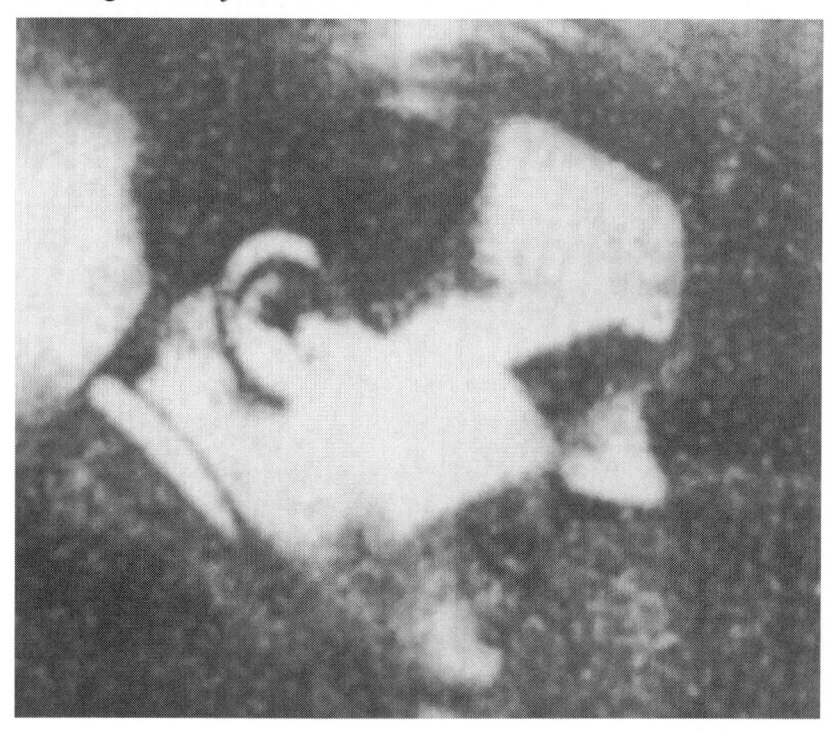

George Francis Shaw leaving the High Court in Glasgow

'But when Lord Thomson informed him in the first few paragraphs of his judgement that his appeal had been disallowed, he sat grim but unmoved during the remainder of the proceedings.'

Mrs Cairns even penned a letter to the Queen protesting her lover's innocence. But it failed to prevent or even delay the inevitable. On January 8, 1953, Shaw's death warrant was issued. A letter from the Office of Public Works to the Governor of Barlinnie instructed that arrangements should be made to have 'the equipment at the prison overhauled and thoroughly oiled and to have a suitable coffin delivered'.

Shaw's execution was scheduled for 8am on January 26. Two days prior to the event, he wrote to his brother John.

'I want you to promise me that you will write home to mother and let her know that I am not afraid to die as I have done no murder,' he instructed.

'I will watch [Sybil] every night and my children to see that nothing will happen to them. I am going to come back and haunt everyone that done me wrong in this dirty world.'

On the morning of the day of his execution, Shaw rose at 6.15am and dressed in his own civilian clothing. He was served a breakfast of porridge and milk, tea, toast and marmalade although ate little, leaving most of the meal.

In a final statement to the Baillie who met him as he walked to the gallows, he said: 'I am as innocent as anyone.'

At 8am, his hands were pinioned to his side and he was escorted the brief distance to the scaffold. Barlinnie's Death Watch Book reveals that he was very calm and composed throughout.

Conducted by Albert Pierrepoint, from Manchester, and assisted by Stephen Wade, from Doncaster, Shaw was executed at 8.01am and the cause of death recorded as 'judicial hanging'. The death sentence was witnessed by two magistrates, the depute town clerk, the governor and medical officer of Barlinnie and a visiting Roman Catholic clergyman.

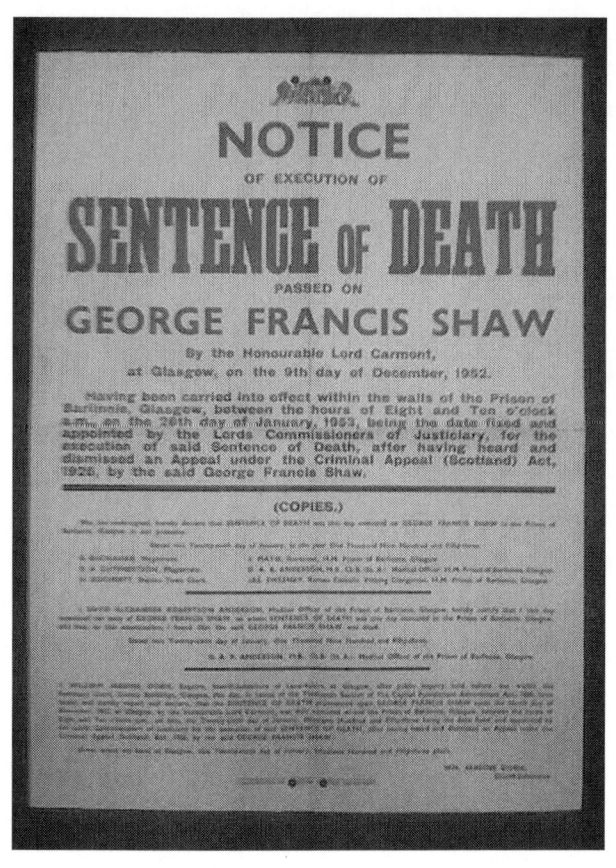

Notice of Execution of Sentence of Death on George Francis Shaw

At 9am, Shaw's body was buried in an unmarked grave in the grounds of the jail.

Later that day, the *Evening Citizen* reported: 'Quietly and calmly protesting his innocence, George Francis Shaw was executed early today.'

While Shaw protested his innocence to the end, the evidence against him, although circumstantial, was persuasive. The socks he was wearing when he was apprehended, the distinctive army coat – which he cherished and frequently wore – and his carefree spending after the death of the old hermit, all linked him to Connelly and his brutal demise. Swift finger pointing by his co-accused Dunn did not help his case. Whether murder was on his mind when the pair headed out to the hut is not known. What is known is that Connelly was said to have kept money aside from his pension to pay for warm winter clothing and a decent burial. Perhaps the pair had simply planned to rob the old man and when he refused to co-operate Shaw, whose upbringing and lifestyle was described as 'rough and unsettled', resorted to violence, battering the frail old man to death in a fit of rage.

Michael Connelly was laid to rest on August 26, 1952, at St Mary's Roman Catholic Cemetery in Lanark, the service attended by nieces and nephews traced during the police inquiry.

*****

9. Peter Manuel

Peter Manuel has gone down in history as one of Scotland's most notorious serial killers. He was convicted of murdering seven people and, on the eve of his execution, confessed to other killings, possibly as many as 18 in total. Well dressed, confident and articulate, he represented himself in court after dismissing his counsel and was even complimented on the 'remarkable' skill with which he defended himself by the judge, Lord Cameron. His behaviour in the condemned cell at Barlinnie Prison, however, contrasted sharply with the relaxed and poised public persona he had previously presented to the world.

Manuel arrived at Barlinnie at 5.56pm on May 29, 1958. Sentenced to death by hanging he was immediately incarcerated within the condemned cell.

While the people of Scotland struggled to comprehend the gruesome scale of his killing spree, he settled down to supper before reading a book. Outside news of his crimes was being conveyed around the world. His trial attracted huge international interest, drawing news reporters from across Britain and the United States. Manuel even tuned into the 9pm news broadcast on his cell radio to hear the verdict before cheerfully returning his attention to his book.

He knew the outcome for just a few hours earlier he had sat in silence as Lord Cameron donned his black triangular cap. The sentence marked the culmination of a 16-day long trial that gripped a nation. In the end it took the jury of nine men and six women a little over two hours to find Manuel guilty of six capital murders and one simple, or non-capital, murder.

Destined to spend his final days at Barlinnie, Manuel's life of crime – which began at the tender age of 11 – had run its course. For two years the people of Lanarkshire had lived in fear, no one knowing where he would strike next. Now there was relief that at last the killer who had lived amongst them and terrorised their neighbourhoods was finally behind bars.

Born in Manhatten, New York, he was the second of three children. His parents, Samuel and Bridget Manuel, upped sticks and moved to America in search of a better life in the 1920s. But his father's ill-heath forced them to return to Scotland and in 1932 they settled briefly in Motherwell before moving south of the border to Coventry.

Peter Manuel

Manuel struggled to fit in at school and frequently played truant. In 1938 he broke into a chapel and stole money from the collection box. Later in the same year he was caught breaking into a shop and a house. He was sent to an approved school but frequently escaped and continued to burgle and steal.

School reports reveal details of these crimes. One stated: 'During one of his abscondings on October 10, 1941, he was caught by the police having broken into a house a few doors from the school and stolen a handbag. The lady of the house saw him coming from her bedroom with an axe in his hand. As a result she had a nervous breakdown. His escapades have alarmed the district.'

In another incident, when he was 15, he committed his first known act of criminal violence.

'On June 10, 1942, he absconded and was charged with three cases of breaking and entering and stealing and one of malicious bodily harm by striking a woman, who was asleep in bed, on the head, causing concussion and haemorrhage. The woman was in hospital for some time. He pled guilty be could give no explanation,' the school reported.

Educational officials were at a loss with what to do with the young Manuel. Another report revealed that he received 'considerable punishment'. But it added: 'The headmaster does not think more of it will reform him.'

Later he was charged with indecently assaulting the wife of one of the school staff. He knocked her on the head with a stick and attempted to rape her. He dragged her to a wood where most of her clothing was removed. Later she was found wandering by a neighbour in a semi conscious state. She required eight stitches to her head and her nose and shoulder bone were broken in the attack.

Manuel pled guilty to robbery with violence. He was also charged with housebreaking and 'wanton damage of an unbelievable nature to the contents of a room, including malicious cutting of bedding and clothing and destroying of foodstuffs.' The scattering of food and cigarette ends was to become a trademark of his future crimes.

He was held for a month in Leeds Prison. His father asked if he could be transferred to an approved school in Scotland but the request was refused. Instead, Manuel was sent to a borstal in Yorkshire for two years. He continued to abscond.

In borstal he was described as 'the world's worst liar' and a 'slippery customer' who 'likes to hear himself talk'.

Upon his release in 1946, 18-year-old Manuel moved north to Lanarkshire where his parents now lived. His offending continued and in February 1946, he was once again caught breaking into a house. While out on bail awaiting trial for this matter, he assaulted three women, raping one of them.

On June 25, at Glasgow High Court he was sentenced to eight years imprisonment for the rape. Incarcerated in Peterhead Prison he expressed resentment over his sentence, claiming that he had been let down by the legal system. He requested law books covering perjury, false arrest and conviction on prejudiced evidence and appears to have spent much time studying the Scottish legal system.

In 1950, in a fit of temper, he threw a load of dishes over a gallery at Peterhead and then smashed 30 panes of glass in the windows. He threatened two officers with the shards of broken glass.

Following this incident, Manuel was examined by a psychiatrist who concluded that he was an 'aggressive psychopath'. The doctor's report added: 'It is doubtful whether, even at the beginning of his sentence, any constructive work could have been done with him.'

The governor of Peterhead described him as a 'very unpleasant type of prisoner' who caused trouble. 'The prisoner is no fool and an absolute pest,' he added.

Manuel was released a year early from Peterhead Prison and returned to the family home in Birkenshaw, Lanarkshire.

He worked briefly, first as a ticket checker with British Railways and then as a labourer with the Scottish Gas Board. In the autumn of 1954 he met a girl, Anne O'Hara. She was a conductress on the bus he took to work. Over time their relationship blossomed and the following year the couple got engaged. However, she refused to marry him on the grounds he would not go to church.

Shortly after the relationship ended, Manuel was back in court, accused of indecently assaulting a woman. After conducting his own defence, he was acquitted.

It was not long, however, before he graduated to murder.

On the afternoon of January 4, 1956, the body of 17-year-old Anne Knielands was found in woodland adjacent to a golf course at East

Kilbride, a new town on the outskirts of Glasgow. The teenager's head had been violently battered and evidence on the ground indicated she had been chased over some distance before being bludgeoned to death at Capelrig Copse. Although she had not been sexually assaulted, stains were found on her clothing, suggesting her killer had reached sexual climax through violence.

Police discovered that on the day the body was discovered, Manuel was working with a group of Scottish Gas Board engineers close to the copse and there were scratch marks on his face. Police interviewed him and some of his clothing was taken away for examination. Manual claimed he was at home on the night of the murder, a story corroborated by his father. He said he got the scratches in a fight on New Year's Eve and the tests on his clothes revealed nothing.

Despite denying any knowledge of the Anne Knielands murder, Manuel remained on the police radar, largely due to the suspicions of Chief Inspector William Muncie.

Two months later officers receive a tip-off that a robbery was to take place at a colliery in Blantyne. A time and date was provided and Manuel was named as one of the two men involved.

The information proved to be accurate and although Manuel managed to escape the awaiting officers, he left incriminating evidence at the scene and was later arrested. He appeared at Hamilton Sheriff Court where a trial date was set and he was granted bail.

In the intervening period, police investigated two house break-ins, both bearing Manual's hallmarks of scattered food and cigarette butts. He also frequently left behind footprints.

On the morning of September 17, officers were called to a bungalow in Fennsbank Avenue, High Burnside. It was just a few doors down the road from one of the two earlier break-ins. Inside they found the bodies of Mrs Marion Watt, her 16-year-old daughter Vivienne and Mrs Watt's sister, Mrs Margaret Brown. All three had been shot dead at close range.

After finding spilled food and discarded cigarette ends, police suspected Manuel and detectives were despatched to his house with a search warrant. Manual refused to answer any of their questions and no clues were found. Eager to make an arrest, officers then turned their attention to Mrs Watt's husband, William, who was away on a fishing trip in Argyll. Police suspected he had driven home under cover of darkness from the hotel he was staying at in Lochgilphead, committed the murders, and then returned north to continue his holiday. It was a heavily flawed theory, but on September 27, Mr Watt was arrested and charged with the murders of his wife, daughter and sister-in-law.

He was remanded to Barlinnie Prison where, by chance, Manuel was starting an 18-month sentence for his part in the attempted robbery at the Blantyre colliery. Manuel took a keen interest in Watt's case, even meeting with Mr Watt's solicitor on a number of occasions. He claimed he knew who committed the murders but refused to divulge the information, either to the brief or police.

It quickly became apparent that Manuel knew rather too much about the incident and with the case against Mr Watt collapsing, he was the prime suspect once again. Unfortunately for investigators there was no hard evidence linking him to any of the murders and the killings continued.

On December 29, 1957, police received a report that 17-year-old Isabelle Cooke, from Mount Vernon, had failed to return home from a dance. A week later, the bodies of Peter Smart, his wife Doris and the couple's 11-year-old son Michael were found in their home in Uddingston. All three victims had been shot in the head at point blank range.

Convinced Manuel was involved, police employed the services of a trusted informant close to him who fed back information while other clues were gathered. A team of 20 men was detailed to keep a 24-hour watch on him. Manuel was witnessed spending cash taken from the Smart house while his father was arrested and charged with handling stolen goods. Items found in the Manuel house – a Kodak camera and a pair of gloves, which Manuel had given to his sister and father as Christmas gifts – were linked to a break-in at a minister's home in Mount Vernon, three days before Isabelle Cooke disappeared.

With his father behind bars at Barlinnie, Manuel offered detectives a deal. He would confess all in return for his father's freedom. The police took some convincing but in the end they agreed and, with his parents present, he described each of the eight killings. He led officers to the field where Isabelle Cooke's body was buried and pointed out the spots on the River Clyde where he disposed of the Webley .38 and Beretta guns used in the Watt and Smart murders respectively. Both were recovered from the water, as was an iron bar used to kill Anne Knielands.

Despite the callous and cold-blooded nature of his killings and the cruelty inflicted on others, Manuel was said to be very fond of his parents and his sister Theresa. He could not bear to see his father incarcerated.

The confessions, along with the other evidence gathered, were sufficient to put Manuel in the dock at the High Court in Glasgow. Securing convictions, however, was another matter. He promptly denied everything and embarked upon a form of defence known as impeachment. From the witness stand, he would accuse others of committing the crimes. This was an unusual step; impeachment had not been employed as a defence in a Scottish murder trial for nearly a century. His defence also relied heavily on alibis.

Crowds gathered in the streets around the High Court as the trial opened on the morning of May 12, 1958. It was considered to be the trial of the decade, if not the century. The courtroom was packed.

The prosecution spent the first two days describing the eight killings and details of Manuel's discussions with Mr Watt's lawyer in Barlinnie were also revealed to the jury.

After attempting to show that William Watt may have shot his own family, Manuel's defence counsel, Harold Leslie QC, argued that his client's verbal and written statements to police should not be admissible as evidence. The judge disagreed and ruled they should be heard in open court. The following day Manuel sacked his lawyer and embarked upon his own defence.

William Watt was again called to the witness box and Manuel repeatedly tried to pin the Watt family murders on him. He also claimed he was framed by police over the Smart murders.

The jury spent two hours and 21 minutes considering 16 days worth of evidence and found Manuel guilty of murdering Marion Watt, Vivienne Watt, Margaret Brown, Peter, Doris and Michael Smart and Isabelle Cook. On Lord Cameron's direction, the jury acquitted him of murdering Anne Kneilands due to a lack of corroborating evidence.

Glasgow Evening Times front page reporting Manuel's conviction

Execution was set for June 19 and Manuel returned to Barlinnie where he had been held on remand in the days leading up to and including the trial. Now, however, he was placed in the condemned cell to await his fate.

His initial spell there was fairly unremarkable. He ate well and spent his time reading, doing crosswords, sketching and listening to the radio. His favourite station was Radio Luxembourg and he had a good knowledge of current hits and the popular artists of the day. Sometimes he would chat with the watch officers. Topics of discussion included his trial, contemporary music and football.

He demanded a newspaper, describing it as his 'favourite reading material' and complained about the books on offer.

'I don't know why I'm being given so many books about the sea,' he said. 'They must think I was a sailor. I prefer books about women.'

Four days into his stay, the prison governor acknowledged his newspaper request and each morning, along with his cigarettes and mail, he was delivered a copy of *The Glasgow Herald*.

Then, on Friday, June 20, his appearance and behaviour changed completely. In the afternoon, the counsel conducting his appeal, Mr R.H. McDonald QC, was due to see him for the first time. However, at 2.20pm, shortly before the lawyer arrived, Manuel was found lying on his back twitching his limbs and frothing at the mouth.

The medical officer was called to the cell and Manuel was immediately transferred to the prison hospital where the contents of his stomach were pumped out.

Initially it was thought that Manuel had attempted to commit suicide. Some believe he tried to kill himself by swallowing toilet cleaner. It is more likely, based on events that followed the incident, that this was simply the beginning of an elaborate rouse designed to convince the authorities that he was insane and should not be hanged for his crimes.

In his report on the incident, governor Mr A.H. Anderson said no evidence of any toxic substance was found and a subsequent analysis of the stomach contents revealed no disinfectant, drugs or soap. He added that no physical cause was found for Manuel's symptoms.

On June 24, *The Glasgow Herald* reported: 'The Scottish Home Department stated last night that an analysis of the contents of Manuel's stomach after his illness on Friday was not yet complete but so far had revealed nothing unusual.'

A Scottish Home Department official added: 'Inquiries in the prison have not revealed the possibility of his having obtained any harmful substance which he could have swallowed.'

Following a thorough search of the condemned cell, Manuel was returned to its confines later the same afternoon. The Condemned Cell Record of Occurrence Book reveals that he lay awake staring at the ceiling. Later he accepted a cigarette but did not speak. He was examined at regular intervals by a doctor and the medical officer and spent a restless night in bed.

The governor wrote: 'Since the episode the prisoner has not spoken either spontaneously or in reply to question. At first he refused food but during the last few days he has taken milk and tea. He spends much of his time crouching on his bed with his legs crossed. He frequently contorts his face, his arms and legs twitch and he takes no apparent interest in his surroundings. He has developed a shuffling gait and his muscular movements are clumsy and abnormal.'

The following morning, watch officers tried repeatedly to give him milk but he refused to take it. He did, however, accept cigarettes.

On the morning of June 22, Manuel sat up in bed at 10.30am and slapped the bed in jerky movements while emitting slight groans, the occurrence book records. At 5.30pm he drank some water but started jerking back and forth, holding his stomach and whimpering. Watch officers observed as his actions became more violent and he struck his head against the wall.

On June 24, amid tight security, Manuel was escorted from Barlinnie to the Appeal Court in Edinburgh. He did not, however, appear in the courtroom and spent the morning in a cell below. His lawyer, Mr R.H. McDonald, said that while Manuel was medically fit both physically and mentally, he considered it not in his client's best interests to be present.

'Before I was instructed on the case he had indicated a desire to be present,' the QC told the judges. 'I have seen him this morning and advised him that in my opinion it is not in his own best interests that he should be present and in the face of that advice he has expressed no further desire to be present.'

Mr McDonald focussed his legal arguments on Lord Cameron's decision to allow Manuel's confession to be heard in open court. He claimed that the arrest and subsequent release of Samuel Manuel on a charge of receiving stolen goods amounted to 'inducement', which would have rendered the confession inadmissible in law.

The Lord Justice-General Clyde ruled that Lord Cameron 'amply justified' the course which he took in allowing the evidence to go before the jury and the appeal was dismissed.

During Manuel's absence from the condemned cell, a new alarm bell was fitted, enabling watch officers to summon help quickly if required. Manuel left the Appeal Court during the lunchtime adjournment and on his return to Barlinnie he consumed a meal of fish and potatoes, the first time he had eaten in four days.

Shortly after midnight, however, he woke, sat up, pounded the bed with his fists, shook his head and uttered what the watch officers described as 'incoherent sounds'.

Later that day, one wrote: 'I'm not sure if prisoner heard the rejection of appeal on the wireless as it was turned down at the time. A few minutes later he sat up and started pulling usual funny faces.'

At 3.45pm on June 25 Manuel was officially informed that his appeal had failed and a new execution date was set for July 11.

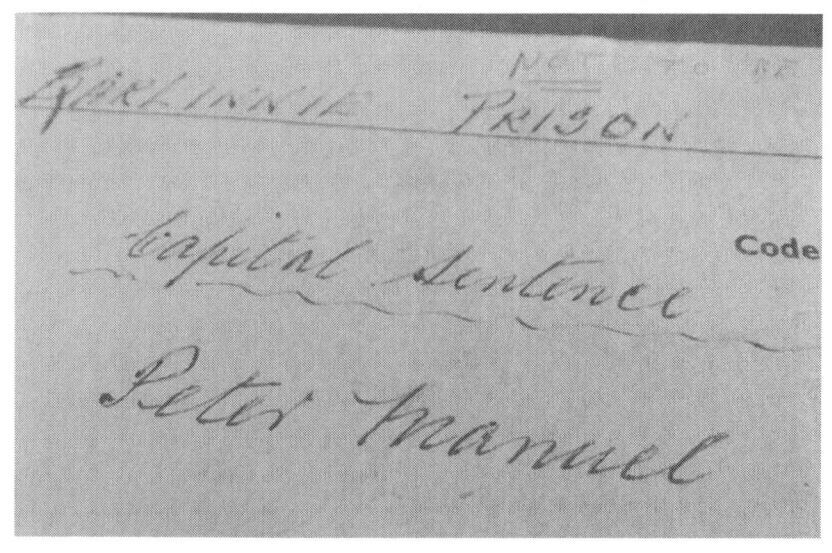

Peter Manuel's Condemned Cell Record of Occurrence Book

'Prisoner quiet but acting queer,' the occurrence book records.

Later entries state: 'Prisoner quiet but always acting strange, twitching his face, arms and body,' and: 'Prisoner quiet but always whimpering and shrugging his shoulders when sitting up on bed.'

On June 29 at 8.25pm he sat up and began throwing his clothes about, moaning and punching his bed with his fist and the following morning he was roused from bed but refused to dress and was 'aggressive, moody and violent at times'.

Manuel refused to speak to his watch officers and did not answer any of their questions. He requested cigarettes by sitting up in bed and uttering the word 'chips'.

On July 6, his parents visited the prison but despite sitting together for almost half an hour he appeared not to recognise them and did not speak.

In the run up to his trial, Manuel was examined 13 times by some of the country's leading psychiatrists and neurologists. None found any reason to declare him insane and unfit to plead in court. Following his conviction, he was again examined on a number of occasions.

Medical Commissioners Dr H.B. Craigie and Dr Laura M.D. Mill concluded that while Manuel was 'abnormal', they did not believe that his responsibility was diminished at the time the crimes were committed.

Their report noted: 'Manual saw himself as an attractive and clever personality, and came to have an exaggerated idea of his abilities and an overweening vanity. He courted the limelight and his ruthless egotism reacted badly and often violently to frustration and authority.

'He never developed an adult sense of responsibility and remained emotionally immature and unable to form satisfactory personal relationships. His morbidly inflated ego was built upon a personality which was fundamentally inadequate.

'He might therefore be expected to crumble following his sentence and the failure of his appeal with the consequent inevitable collapse of his self-confidence.'

The doctors attempted to interview Manuel at Barlinnie on June 26. The meeting lasted for 30 minutes during which time Manuel said nothing and refused to answer any of their questions.

They were not, however, fooled by the sudden change in his appearance and behaviour that began on June 20.

'In our opinion, and after careful consideration of all the circumstances of his case and previous information available to us, the symptoms that he now displays have been more consciously than sub consciously developed,' the doctors reported. In short, he was putting it on.

'Many prisoners believe that there are advantages to be gained by simulating insanity as a method, for example, of evading a prison sentence. We have no doubt that Manuel – an astute and intelligent man – is well aware of these possibilities and that he might think that a convincing and suitably dramatic display of symptoms of mental disorder would be well within his capacity and could be of use to him.'

It would come as no surprise to them therefore that with both appeal and reprieve rejected, Manuel gave up his insanity charade on July 10 – the day before his execution. He started to talk again and the occurrence book reveals that he was 'very cheerful and talkative and conversed continually about his trial and appeal and appeared in good spirits'.

After a last supper of fish, chips, lettuce, tomatoes, bread and tea, he was escorted to the prison control room where he was met by the governor for what was officially described as an 'interview'. It is believed that during this two-hour session, Manuel confessed to a series of unsolved murders.

He returned to the condemned cell at 7.45pm and after a visit by his older brother James at 8.10pm, he remained awake for most of the night. At 4am on the morning of his execution he read through old letters before destroying them.

Manuel spent the remainder of the night sitting at the table in the cell playing dominoes and listening to the radio. At 6.25am he washed and changed into his civilian clothes before, at 6.50am, he heard

Mass and took Holy Communion in an empty cell adjacent to the condemned cell where an altar had been set up.

Manuel returned to the condemned cell at 7.25am where the medical officer, David Anderson, gave him a large glass of whisky. He sat with a visiting Roman Catholic chaplain until 7.58am when the governor and executioner Harry Allen entered the cell. While Allen strapped his arms down, Manuel spoke briefly with the governor, expressing his thanks to the staff that had looked after him. He told the hangman: 'Turn up the radio and I'll go quietly.'

A minute later he was escorted across the gallery and at 8am he was hanged.

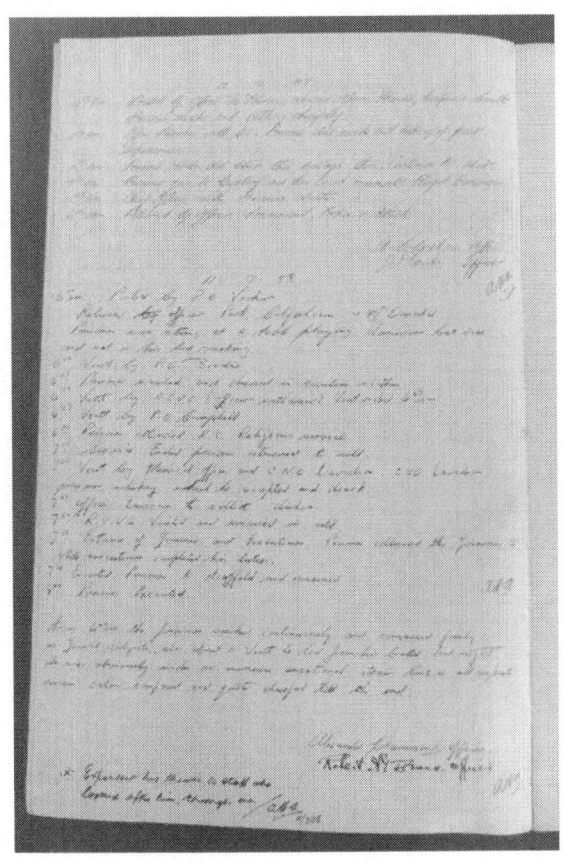

Final page of Peter Manuel's Condemned Cell Record of Occurrence Book

One of the watch officers observed: 'From 6am the prisoner smoked continuously and conversed freely on general subjects, also about a visit he had from his brother last night. He was obviously under an immense emotional strain but in all respects remained calm, composed and quite cheerful till the end.'

His crimes left a lasting impression both on Scotland and on the English language – he was the first mass murderer in the world to be labelled a 'serial killer'.

*****

10. Anthony Joseph Miller

In the 1950s and 60, Queen's Park was a popular recreational area well used by the people of Glasgow's Govan district, clean open space amid the grimy urban sprawl where men and boys played football on the ash pitches, families picnicked on the grass and couples wandered aimlessly around the network of paths. By night, however, the area had an altogether murkier and more squalid reputation. Unbeknown to many, it was a notorious haunt for homosexual men.

Two young lads who were well aware of what was going on in the park after darkness fell were Anthony Miller and James Denovan. They were frequent visitors. But neither was looking for sex. Instead, they made a living, albeit an unlawful one, robbing unwary gay men.

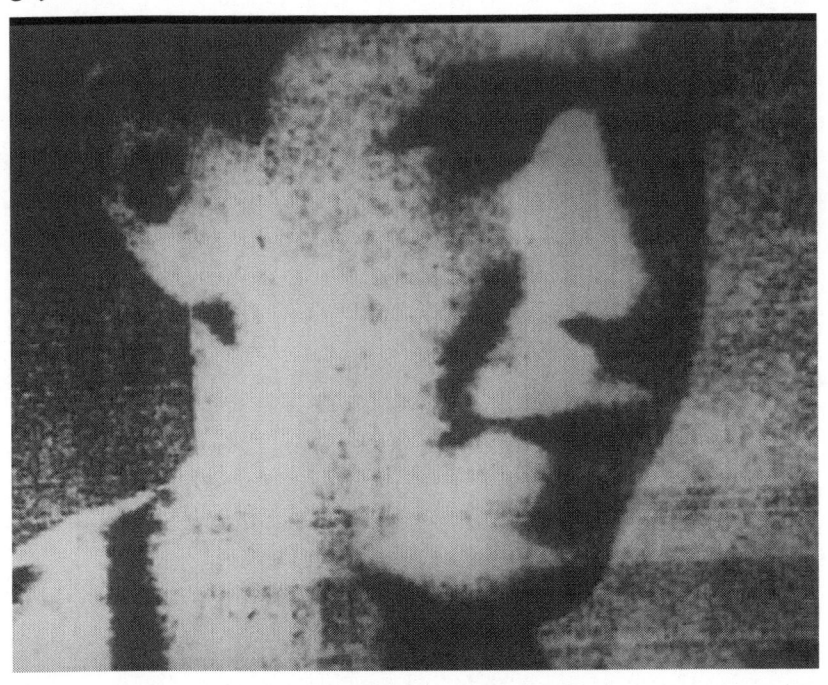

Anthony Miller

Miller, a 19-year-old apprentice cabinetmaker who worked in the removals industry, first encountered 16-year-old Denovan in the Cathkin Café in Cathcart Road. They quickly struck up a rapport and met regularly, chatting, laughing and playing records on the café's jukebox.

Both came from decent, hard-working families and both lived in comfortable homes near the park. But despite good upbringings, they were not good boys. Miller, it was reported, had a fascination with fascism and modelled himself on a Nazi storm trooper. He kept a scrapbook charting the life of his hero, Adolf Hitler, and claimed his real name was 'Muller', the German spelling.

Together, he and Denovan ran amuck, daubing swastikas and other fascist graffiti on walls and buildings. In time they hatched a more sinister plan to make some easy money from the illicit nocturnal activities in Queen's Park.

Denovan would act as a decoy, a smiling, fresh-faced youngster who hung around the public toilets and lured men to secluded spots where Miller, who pretended to be drunk, struck, assaulting and robbing them.

They were not alone. Across the park, men were being mugged on a regular basis. It was a practice known as 'queer rolling' and, as homosexuality was illegal at the time, very few incidents were reported to the police.

It was a profitable scam and for almost a year the pair targeted a steady stream of victims, lined their pockets with their ill-gotten gains. However, on April 6, 1960, things went too far.

John Cremin, a 48-year-old homosexual, general dealer and small time crook, was staying in a hotel close to the park. Newspapers reported that he told people he had travelled through from Dundee to attend a football match at Hampden Park. In reality, he hailed from Glasgow and rather than heading across the recreational area to the stadium, he was in fact going there in search of gay sex.

Cremin thought he had found what he was looking for when he bumped into Denovan. The 16-year-old invited him to accompany him to a more secluded spot and Cremin duly followed.

Queen's Park Recreational Area

However, when they reached an area sheltered by bushes, Miller leapt out from his hiding place and ambushed Cremin. A brutal attack followed, Miller beating him repeatedly on the head with a plank of wood. Denovan rifled Cremin's pockets and the pair made off with a bankbook, a watch, a knife and £67 in cash.

Leaving Cremin's battered body lying in the undergrowth, they celebrated their haul by buying drinks with the stolen £5 notes. It is said that Miller even lit a cigarette with one of the fivers. The following night, money still burning a hole in their pockets, they splashed out on a trip to the cinema, buying two tickets for Tommy The Toreador, a musical starring Tommy Steele.

As they sat in the picture house, a man walking his dog found Cremin's body. With a cap concealing severe head injuries, it was initially thought he had fallen and died of natural causes. However, a post mortem carried out by two of the country's most respected pathologists, James Rentoul and Walter Pollock Weir, revealed he had been murdered. They were in no doubt that a heavy blow from an object with a flat surface, such as a piece of wood, caused the fatal injury.

Detectives immediately launch an investigation and, in a bid to trace relatives of Cremin, an appeal was published in the Press. Denovan read the report, cut it out and put it in his wallet.

The murder and police hunt did not put a stop to their activities and throughout the summer of 1960 Miller and Denovan continued to target men in the park. In August, however, Denovan was caught performing a sex act on a man in a public toilet. Officers searched him and found the Cremin newspaper cutting in his back pocket.

He was arrested and questioned. Detained in a remand home in Edinburgh Road he confessed all to his father and gave police a statement telling how he and Miller had carried out a series of attacks on homosexuals in Queen's Park and one of them had died.

Miller was brought in for questioning and the pair subsequently appeared side by side in the dock at Glasgow Sheriff Court charged with the murder of John Cremin.

Miller's father, Alf Miller, hired Glasgow lawyer Len Murray to defend his son. He said the evidence against the pair was overwhelming.

'The evidence implicating Miller and Denovan in the murder charge came from several sources,' Murray continued.

'The pair had been in the habit of frequenting the Cathkin Cafe in Victoria Road in Glasgow's Southside. A number of their friends had told the police how Miller and Denovan had often boasted in the cafe of what they had done to Cremin.

'Some of them even spoke of one ghoulish moment when the two accused pointed out the very spot in the Recreation Ground where Cremin had been assaulted and had 'flaked' in their words. Denovan had suggested that they observe two minutes' silence for him.

'Miller and Denovan had also been seen in possession of Cremin's bank book and they had also been seen with new bank notes.'

As murder in the course of furtherance of theft remained a capital crime, Murray knew all too well that if Miller were convicted he would hang. Denovan was too young to face the gallows.

The trial, before Lord Wheatley, got underway at the High Court in Glasgow on November 14. Miller and Denovan both denied that on April 6, 1960, in Queen's Park Recreation Ground, Glasgow, they assault John Cremin and struck him on the head with a piece of wood or other similar instrument, knocked him down and robbed him of a bank book, a watch, a knife and £67 of money, and murdered him.

The pair also faced charges relating to other assaults and robberies.

Murray recalled: 'By the second day of the trial the issue had become confined to only the capital charge because both Miller and Denovan tendered pleas of guilty to all the other charges.

'Indeed the issue had become even more narrow – which of the two of them had struck John Cremin on that fateful night? This was crucial because in terms of the Homicide Act of 1957 only the one whose hands had dealt the fatal blow could be hanged.'

Giving evidence in his own defence, Denovan claimed that Miller was the one who brandished the length of wood. He said that he had no idea that Miller was going to strike such a severe blow and while he did not mind being party to an assault, he did not want any unnecessary violence.'

In court, Detective Inspector James McLaren, the officer who interviewed Denovan in the remand house, read out the statement he had taken from the teenager.

'The night that the man died was a Wednesday night,' Denovan's account began. 'I picked him up and went round the side of the toilet. The man was smelling of drink. He was smaller than me and was wearing a loose raincoat and cloth cap. He was between 40 and 50 and stockily built.

'Miller came round and stood a bit away and was stotting around acting drunk. Just me and Miller were there.

'The man was touching me. I said to him: "Let us move off and go over to the air raid shelters at the Grange Road end".

'We moved towards Miller and the man looked at Miller as we passed.

'I said to the man: "He is drunk".

'Well, we just passed and out of the corner of my eye I saw Miller pick up a bit of wood about three and a half feet long. He just stepped forward and hit the man on the back of the head with it. The man had both hands in his pockets and he just fell straightforward.

'We both bent over him, and I took his wristwatch off and put it in my pocket. Miller pulled one of the man's hands out of his pocket and he had an open penknife in it.

'We rolled him over on his face and I pulled a big bundle of notes out of his hip pocket. Miller was going through his pockets and got a bankbook.

'A couple of people, I think two men, were standing watching us and Miller was lifting the man up to let them think we were trying to help a drunk man.'

Denovan then described their route from the park to the tenement close where Miller lived. Within the confined of the stairwell, Miller counted the money.

'There were quite a number of new £1 notes and he gave me five of them. He was dealing the notes out like cards, five at a time,' Denovan's statement continued.

'We divided the money equally. I got £33 10s and he got the same. I got the watch and I think I pawned it later.'

Miller gave no evidence at the trial.

In his summing up to the jury, prosecutor Advocate-depute James Law said: 'I do not suggest in this case that Miller intended to kill. My case is that Miller, along with Denovan, was engaged in a criminal enterprise, was out to use violence to further his own criminal ends. I invite you to hold that that is, in fact, murder.

'Although it was not done deliberately, it was done in the furtherance of this criminal enterprise regardless of the probable consequences.'

The jury of nine men and six women took just 35 minutes to convict Miller and Denovan of the murder. Miller knew what was coming and the Press covering the trial reported that there were tears in his eyes and he lost all colour in his face when he heard the sentence.

The *Evening Times* reported: 'The atmosphere in the High Court was electric when the jury returned this afternoon a finding that both youths were guilty of the killing of John Cremin.

'When the foreman of the jury uttered the fatal words, Denovan, the baby-faced bespectacled 16-year-old, hung his head and reddened.

'But Miller, the man sentenced to die, stared straight ahead at the judge, his face impassive – until after a moment or two, a hard smile parted his lips.'

Passing sentence on Miller, Lord Whealey said: 'In respect of the verdict of capital murder just received, for which the law imposes but one sentence, the sentence of the court is that you be taken from this place to the prison of Barlinnie, therein to be detained until December 7, and on that date within said prison, between the hours of eight o'clock and 10 o'clock, you will suffer death by hanging.'

The Glasgow Evening Times report of the verdict

There was a stillness in the court, the *Evening Times* report continued, while the black cap was produced. Placing it lightly on his head Lord Wheatley uttered the final words of the sentence: 'which is pronounced for doom.'

Miller was quickly hustled from the dock and Denovan then stood up to receive his sentence. Convicted of non-capital murder due to his age, he was ordered by Lord Wheatley to be detained at Her Majesty's Pleasure indefinitely.

As Miller headed off to the condemned cell at Barlinnie Prison, the conclusion of the trial prompted an outpouring of lurid headlines from the tabloid newspapers of the day, much of it focussing on the sexual activities of late night visitors to Queen's Park.

The *Daily Express*, for example, described the court proceedings as: 'the trial that shocked all Scotland with its squalid revelations of homosexual vice.'

Lord Wheatley himself touched upon the subject in his address to the jury, commenting: 'There is a background of vice, depravity and violence which may have shocked and astonished you.'

It may have shock some but so-called 'queer rolling' and attacks on men looking for sex in the park – either gay or straight – were nothing new. Miller and Denovan were not the first to kill a man there. In the 1920s Albert Fraser (24) and James Rollins (23) used female friends to lure men to a quiet spot where they were robbed. On one occasion, the pair kicked a 35-year-old man to death. Both were hanged.

The so-called 'revelations' prompted Glasgow's civic councillors into action. Baillie J.G. McNair demanded that Queen's Park be completely enclosed and shut to the public at dusk each day while others called for lights to be installed along the two paths bisecting the recreation area.

After picking through the spoils of the case, Murray lodged an appeal. But he held out little hope of success.

'We were not optimistic about our chances in the Appeal Court,' he said. 'It was a hard line court and only a tiny proportion of criminal appeals ever had any success. It was the last resort in Scotland and, unlike England, there was and is no appeal to the House of Lords in criminal matters.'

He believed Miller stood a better chance of a reprieve and the condemned man's father, a merchant seaman, collected nearly 30,000 signatures calling for his son's life to be spared.

'The petition for reprieve was another matter. It had to succeed. There was every reason to think that it would. Tony Miller was only 19. He had never previously offended. He came from a good home. No member of his family had ever been in any bother and the killing was obviously not premeditated,' Murray said.

The lawyer visited his client once a week in prison and found a man increasingly more resigned to his fate.

'I found those to be strange meetings. He seemed to be becoming more distant or perhaps more resigned. Sometimes I felt as though he was not very interested in whether the appeal succeeded or not, or even whether the petition was successful or not.

'His attitude was that if it were the will of God then he would be reprieved. If it were not God's will then it would not happen. I found this an extraordinary attitude in one so young. In those weeks following his conviction Tony Miller was acquiring a maturity far beyond his years.'

Miller's appeal was rejected and a new date – December 22 – was set for his execution. His family and lawyer, however, had not given up and their hopes for clemency were buoyed following the reprieve on December 16 of 25-year-old Robert Dickson.

Dickson, an assistant lighthouse keeper, had killed relief lighthouse keeper Hugh Clark at Little Ross lighthouse, off the south west coast of Scotland, and was convicted of capital murder and theft at the High Court in Dumfries. He was sentenced to death but this was reduced to life imprisonment following the intervention of the then Secretary of State for Scotland, John Maclay.

In Miller's case, however, the Scottish Secretary, who cut short a holiday to consider the matter, found himself unable to find sufficient grounds to 'justify him in advising the Queen to interfere with the due course of the law'.

The news was broken to Miller in the death cell and to his parents Alf and Marie Miller, who were visiting the prison at the time, within the gatehouse at Barlinnie.

The *Daily Express* reported: 'There, at 3.30pm, they handed over the letter to Governor Harry Anderson. He went with them to the death cell. Slim, dark haired Miller and two wardens were waiting.

'Baillie Brown read the letter as Miller stood, staring straight ahead, hands clenched at his side. A minute or two earlier his parents and 21-year-old brother, Paul, had been chatting with him.'

Alf Miller said afterwards, 'Although we were there for 30 minutes there wasn't much said. Tony seemed to be quite cheerful and kept telling his mother not to worry.'

The family made a final appeal direct to the Queen, the telegram drafted by Mrs Miller. 'We the parents of Anthony Joseph Miller, condemned to die on Thursday, December 22, implore your most gracious Majesty to save our son's life,' she wrote.

But there was no reply from Buckingham Palace.

A letter from the assistant governor to the governor at Barlinnie reveals that Miller was visited for the last time by his parents and his brother at 6.15pm on December 21. The meeting lasted for around 45 minutes.

'The visit was most restrained and less emotional than the previous day,' the assistant governor noted.

'Anthony repeatedly said it was not the fault of anyone but himself; he was quite resigned and they were not to worry as he was not unduly concerned. He stressed repeatedly the fact that he had always claimed he would die before his 21st birthday. He told his parents that his present position was the result of his own foolishness.

'On the father stating he would carry on with his efforts to have the death penalty abolished, Anthony intimated his full agreement. He was, however, quick to point out that no grudge should be held against the Secretary of State, who was only doing his duty.'

In a final letter to his father, the teenager wrote: 'I hope that you will take an interest in getting hanging stopped as I wouldn't like to see any other parents suffer the same as you all have done.'

With the execution equipment already in place, executioner Harry Allen and assistant Robert Stewart arrived at the prison on December 21 to make their preparations for Miller's date with destiny.

The following morning, at two minutes past eight, the 19-year-old died at the end of a rope. It is said that as the noose was secured around a tearful Miller's neck he uttered one final plea to the hangman: 'No, please mister, no…'

He was the last person to be hanged at Barlinnie and the last teenager to be executed in Britain.

Confirming his death, a prison spokesman said: 'He was very composed and there was no trouble at all.'

The case highlighted the growing public outrage and opposition to the continued existence of the death penalty. Len Murray was amongst those for whom capital punishment no longer had a place in civilised society.

'Until the Miller case I had probably been in favour of capital punishment,' he said. 'But I realised that this case had made me a bitter abolitionist. The barbarity and the futility of it all were inconsistent with our claims to be a civilised society.

'Not only were they going to destroy a life that should be saved, a life that did not belong to them, but in addition a punishment far greater than any other that man could ever possibly devise was being handed out to two innocent individuals – the parents of the condemned boy.

'To those who say it is a deterrent, I say it is not. I have never seen any evidence from any country in the world that shows capital punishment is a deterrent.

'The great majority of murders, in my experience, are committed in the heat of a moment. Possible punishment is the farthest thing from the mind of the killer.'

For the final time in the prison's history, the Execution Box was packaged up and sent back to Wandsworth Prison in London.

In a letter dated December 22 to the governor there, Barlinnie's governor wrote: 'I return herewith two keys of the equipment which you forwarded here on November 21, 1960. The other equipment will be forwarded by passenger train tomorrow marked "Box of Ropes". Rope No. 10 was used once only.'

*****

Postscript

After the demise of Anthony Miller, only more one judicial hanging took place in Scotland. In 1963, Henry John Burnett (21) was executed at Craiginches Prison, Aberdeen, following his conviction for the murder of seaman Thomas Guyan.

In 1965, under the Murder (Abolition of Death Penalty) Act, hanging was suspended for an experimental period of five years.

On December 16, 1969 the House of Commons, followed two days later by the House of Lords, voted to abolish the death penalty for murder permanently, although it remained on the Statute Book for treason, piracy with violence and arson in Royal Dockyards.

Two years later, the crime of arson in Royal Dockyards was scrapped and in 1998, the Criminal Justice Bill removed treason and piracy with violence as capital crimes, effectively ending capital punishment in the UK.

In the same year, MPs voted to adopt provisions contained within the European Convention on Human Rights outlawing capital punishment for murder except 'in times of war or imminent threat of war' and incorporated the European Convention on Human Rights into British law.

In 1999 Britain signed the sixth protocol of the European Convention of Human Rights, formally abolishing the death penalty in the UK and ensuring it could not be brought back.

The hanging shed at Barlinnie remained in situ until 1995 when plans were drawn up to demolish it as part of a major renovation of D-Hall.

At the time, the deputy governor of Barlinnie, Mrs Kate Donegan, described the facility as a 'total anachronism' with no place in modern penal thinking.

'Over the years it has been a closed-off part of the prison which everyone was aware was there but which no-one really thought about,' she added.

The condemned cell ended its days as a storage room for cleaning materials, bins, buckets and chamber pots.

Although the execution suite had not been used since 1960, it was maintained because capital punishment remained on the Statute Book and Scotland was required to retain a facility.

There was also the possibility, however unlikely, that the government's stance on capital punishment for murder might change at some point in the future.

As part of D-Hall's £5.2 million upgrade all traces of the hanging shed and condemned cell disappeared. The old Victorian hall was divided into four smaller units, each capable of accommodating 50 men. Toilets were installed in the new cells, ending the long outdated tradition of 'slopping out' in D-Hall (although the practice continued in other parts of the prison until 2002).

During the renovation, which was complete by 1997, the remains of the 10 men hanged at Barlinnie and buried on ground adjacent to D-Hall were exhumed for reburial elsewhere on the prison estate. To this day the bodies remain the property of the State.

Today, Barlinnie is Scotland's largest prison and it holds all categories of prisoners. While its primary role is to detain remand and short-term prisoners sent by courts in the west of Scotland, there are a significant number of newly sentenced long term prisoners who are either awaiting transfer to another establishment or are there for a specific management reason.

The prison has a capacity of just over 1000 but frequently accommodates much higher numbers.

With Barlinnie's hanging shed consigned to history, two execution suites remained in Scotland, one at Perth Prison and the other at Saughton Prison in Edinburgh. In 1999 both were rendered obsolete with the signing of the sixth protocol of the European Convention of Human Rights.

In 2003, the gallows at Saughton were removed and rebuilt as a museum piece at Stirling Old Town Jail, a popular visitor attraction.

*****

Acknowledgements

I would like to thank the friendly, helpful and efficient staff of the National Archives of Scotland in Edinburgh for all their help and assistance in sourcing and retrieving files and documents. Thanks also go to staff at the National Library of Scotland, Edinburgh, for their assistance in accessing newspaper archives. A number of publications were consulted during the research for this book, including *The Glasgow Herald/The Herald, Evening Times, The Bulletin, Evening Citizen, Edinburgh Evening Despatch, Evening News, Scottish Daily Express, Daily Mail* and *Daily Record.*

*****

Printed in Great Britain
by Amazon.co.uk, Ltd.,
Marston Gate.